# Praise

'*Performing Memories and Weaving Archives* is a tour de force exemplar of transdisciplinary scholarship. Sayan Dey painstakingly challenges reductionism through revealing the complex story of African Indians in India and Indian Africans in Africa alongside the many erasures Euromodern colonial practices and rationalizations imposed upon both. From the opening examination of the power of being greeted by strangers in one's own language and the generous act of learning involved in linguistic and other cultural practices of reciprocity, the power of communicative practices, and their creolizing effect—all cultural encounters flow, after all, in many directions and in many ways—Dey offers a provocative methodological framework, through demonstration, in which spiritual memory, music and dance, the joys of culinary memory—in a word, life—and the ever-crucial resistance of reclaimed and transformed humanity come to the fore with breathtaking clarity. Every page is a proverbial gem.'

*Lewis R. Gordon, Professor, Board of Trustees Distinguished Professor and Global Affairs, University of Connecticut, United States, and the Author of* Freedom, Justice, and Decolonization *and* Fear of Black Consciousness

'The book pushes us with delight and dexterity into the world of moving cultures and cultures in motion, where being in cultures is being creolized. Dey is a buoyant, moving citizen as he "senses" experiences across borders, seas, communities, territories, food, music, and the rest, making for an inviting weave.'

*Ranjan Ghosh, the Author of* The Plastic Turn *and* Thinking Literature Across Continents *(with J. Hillis Miller)*

'Dr. Dey welcomes us on a journey of diasporic meanderings as he travels through time, space, geographies, cultural encounters, and hidden histories to explore. Dey also explores how and why invisibilizations are a part of yesterday's colonial Master narrative and today's postcolonial enterprise, both rooted in global anti-Blackness.'

*Dr. Irma McClaurin, Anthropologist and Founder of Irma McClaurin Black Feminist Archive, United States*

'Weaving together rich literary and historical sources, Dey builds a compelling argument on the performative power of greetings by exploring transoceanic interconnections and its resultant creolization between India and South Africa through a multi-sited lens of indigenous memories and spirituality.'

*Dr. Papia Sengupta, Faculty, Centre for Political Studies, Jawaharlal Nehru University, India*

'A timely intervention, *Performing Memories and Weaving Archives* brings the suppressed and marginalized Creole communities back to the center stage of history. Sayan Dey calls attention to our biases and discriminations and argues for a wider recognition of the border crossing groups. Mediating through rituals, music, language, and food practices, the book successfully demonstrates that Creole is actually the norm rather than exception. A great contribution to reshape our understanding of historical cultural practices.'

*Dr. Kuan-Hsing Chen, National Chiao Tung University, the Author of*
Asia as Method: Towards Deimperialization

'*Performing Memories and Weaving Archives* is an enchanting and informative medley of voices at once, primal, and quite contemporary. It evokes transoceanic ties between India and South Africa, especially in music, food, and the sacred. These are stories of transcendence in everyday immanence, showing the triumphant spirit of Ubuntu against the imposition of historical fences.'

*Dr. Devarakshanam Govinden, Academic, Poet, and Historian, South Africa*

'Weaving complex questions about social relations between people in South Africa and India, Sayan Dey provides a provocation to readers: Who are you? Who am I? How are we related? A must read for understanding race, power, and nation in contemporary times.'

*Dr. Melanie Bush, Professor of Sociology, Adelphi University, United States*

'Deploying decolonial perspective as both an overarching conceptual framework and a methodology mixing it with creolization as an analytical unit, Sayan Dey's *Performing Memories and Weaving Archives* enlightens us than never before on the lives and histories of African Indians in India and Indian Africans in South Africa. Dey opens the analytical canvas wide to cover spiritualities, culinary traditions, music, and politics. The shelf life and indeed virtual life of this book on the burgeoning Indian Ocean studies is secured and guaranteed.'

*Dr. Sabelo J. Ndlovu-Gatsheni is Chair of Epistemologies of the Global South and Vice-Dean of Research in the Africa Multiple Cluster of Excellence, University of Bayreuth, Germany*

'Sayan Dey's study of interreligiosities and oceanic human landscapes unearths a tacitly shared history between South Asia and South and East Africa in research uniquely placed at the grassroots level of Afro-Indian and Indo-African subalternities. Exploring their cultural expressions and religious practices, fresh insights into community resilience and adaptation to displacement and migration unfold. Dey compellingly explores the notions of creolization and oceanic cultures as pathways to decolonizing knowledge on (post)colonized communities, mirroring each other in their amalgamation of migration and indigeneity. This is commendable research of Global South–South exchange, unconcerned with global northern hegemonies and epistemologies. Dey engages the reader in the complex and rich realities of subaltern communities and their resistance to casteism and racism, concluding with a call to rewind the erasure of their histories from both Indian and South African national memory and heritage.'

*Dr. Ophira Gamliel, Lecturer, Theology and Religious Studies,*
*University of Glasgow, Scotland*

'In this riveting cultural history, Sayan Dey's explorations of religion, music, dance, and culinary crossings between Africa and India offer much food for thought. A unique investigation of how African and Indian cultures have informed each other over many centuries, *Performing Memories and Weaving Archives* offers a decolonial contribution to many fields, from food studies to musicology to religious studies. Extensively researched and thoughtfully written, this book will command the attention of global historians, Indian Ocean historians, and all those interested in the detailed linkages between Africa and India in the past and continuing into the present.'

*Dr. Neilesh Bose, Associate Professor and Canada Research Chair,*
*Department of History, University of Victoria, Canada*

# Performing Memories and Weaving Archives

# Performing Memories and Weaving Archives

## Creolized Cultures across the Indian Ocean

Sayan Dey

ANTHEM PRESS

Anthem Press
An imprint of Wimbledon Publishing Company
*www.anthempress.com*

This edition first published in UK and USA 2024
by ANTHEM PRESS
75–76 Blackfriars Road, London SE1 8HA, UK
or PO Box 9779, London SW19 7ZG, UK
and
244 Madison Ave #116, New York, NY 10016, USA

*British Library Cataloguing-in-Publication Data*
A catalogue record for this book is available from the British Library.

*Library of Congress Cataloging-in-Publication Data*
A catalog record for this book has been requested.
2023942533

ISBN-13: 978-1-83998-690-1 (Pbk)
ISBN-10: 1-83998-690-5 (Pbk)

Cover Credit: A Creolized Ocean image - courtesy/copyright Sayan Dey

This title is also available as an e-book.

Dedicated to my transoceanic ancestors who always bless me in spirit

# CONTENTS

# FOREWORD

*Performing Memories and Weaving Archives* offers an insightful and rare glimpse of a two-way excavation entailing an Indian Ocean world at the crossroads. Here, the lifeworlds, ancestral knowledge, and collective memories of diasporic African communities in India and conversely diasporic Indian communities in South Africa are put into conversation. The spatiotemporal encounters Dey and his participant authors trace bear upon everyday life through these historic reverberations. This work deftly interweaves three spheres of everyday life: sacredscapes (through the spiritual mnemonic), musicscapes (through cultures of dance, music, and movement), and foodscapes (through culinary practices).

These traversals weave the ancestral knowledge, "creolization," and "decolonial resistance" that thematically braid the multistranded narratives of South African Indians, Siddis, and other Afro-Indian communities. For a narrative that is intensely personal as much as it remains socioculturally expansive and open-ended, Dey begins with his own intergenerational biography against a seemingly familiar backdrop of postindependence Bangladesh and West Bengal in flux. Yet, against the urban fabric of childhood spaces, the portrait of a more muted, intriguing history emerges. It is that of a 15th century African kingdom in West Bengal, the Habshi dynasty, and one of many Afro-Indian kingdoms that dotted precolonial India, and long before Indian indentured labor was shipped across the farthest reaches of the British Empire. It is through these transoceanic and transcontinental interstices that Dey ferrets back and forth, between the historic and the contemporary, in offering readers an "archive of creolized memories."

How is the Indian Ocean as a material space, metaphor, and archive of both connection and dissonance, reimagined in Dey's transoceanic, transcontinental multi-sited ethnography? If a post-Purcellian reading of the so-called Indian Ocean as a transcultural borderland proves useful at some stage, at what point in this tracing of littoral lifeworlds do notions of hybridity, flow, and entanglement get ruptured, if ever? Indeed, Dey and his collaborators prompt us to think with/through the many sensibilities of porosity that pattern diasporic meaning-making and sentiments of belonging. For example, through an intersectional reading of identity and social hierarchy implicating class, caste, gender, and regional communalism among others, they further venture on to complicating contemporary paradoxes of colorism on either side of the Indian Ocean.

Through the mystical, the musical, and the flavorful, Dey's work illustrates how "being there" and connecting seemingly disparate histories and geographies reveal trajectories of intersecting creolization—whether it be through linguistic creolization as evidenced through sung *zikrs*, or culinary creolization as seen in *breyani* with madumbi curry made from South African yam. At the same time however, this kind of tracework also ruptures narratives of linear flow, for rituals encompassing firewalking and spirit possession are seen to be commonly shared between diverse collectives in South Africa and along the Swahili coast, including the Zulu and the Bantu.

Taken together, this work stands as an invaluable contribution to similar crossroads studies/post-area studies thinking, alongside historic work that continues to inspire new thalassology and transoceanic scholarship. Given Dey's background as a literary scholar, what could be said of this form and style of tracework in which vivid metaphor, memories of kinship, and multisensory encounters, alongside practices of exchange and representation are brought together? What in fact, are the "archives" that are being woven here? And, in what form and in whose presence might this radical (re) weaving unfold? This expansively rich contribution also serves as an open invitation to new generations of interdisciplinary scholars, for thinking across and beyond diverse epistemic boundaries and dualisms of place, space and temporality: the ancestral and the creolized, the material and the mnemonic, of transcultural connectivity and rupture, of change and continuity.

**Rapti Siriwardane-de Zoysa**
Senior Researcher
Department of Social Sciences
Leibniz Centre for Tropical Marine Research, Germany

# PREFACE

The evolution of this book is widely motivated by my close association with coastal cultures and oceanic values since my childhood days. I was born in the city of Kolkata, and it is located in the coastal state of West Bengal. As a result, my social, cultural, political, historical, esthetic, and intellectual evolution is deeply entangled and interwoven with diverse coastal cultures, traditions, and lifestyles that are habitually brought into the mainstream, exclusionary, and capitalistic urban cultural spaces of Kolkata by the vegetable vendors, fishmongers, and domestic helpers. A large number of vendors and helpers in Kolkata belong to the coastal regions of West Bengal, and they come to the city in search of jobs. In the process of seeking and engaging in variety of jobs, they not only influence the economic structures of the city, but also transform the culturescapes through their unique spiritual, culinary, musical, societal, fashion, and other practices. For instance, as a child I remember that there were a lot of women in our locality who were from the coastal region of Digha[1] and worked as cooks in different houses. As I had many friends, I would often be invited for lunch or dinner in their houses, and I would be served with traditional coastal dishes of sea fishes, fish eggs, and various other seafood that were prepared by the cooks. Apart from seafood, the cooks would also prepare various other vegetarian and nonvegetarian dishes that are culturally and traditionally rooted in other parts of West Bengal. In this way, I developed a multicultural palate, which allowed me to indulge in an interconnected mode of belonging beyond the narrow enclaves of sociocultural binaries.

Gradually, as I started critically engaging with various oceanic and transoceanic communities and their cultures across India and the world, the collectivity, reciprocity, and malleability of the oceans and their impact on the communities near and far from the coasts, motivated me to embrace a critical, intellectual, esthetic, porous, and fluid identity of "Oceania" that "seeks to open up different ways of being with others, relating, and dwelling in and across this ocean-interconnected world" (Wilson 2022, p. 5).

This identity has served as the inceptual point of this book. Being an oceanian, my personal existence and my research deeply acknowledge that my individual identity has been molded through a consistent process of "archipelagic belonging and transoceanic worlding" (Wilson, p. 5), where the oceans and the humans interact and interact with each other.

Irrespective of our geographical and topographical locationalities, the theoretical, methodological, epistemological, and ontological (Hofmeyr 2021; Menon et al. 2022) impacts of oceans in terms of culinary cultures, food habits, commercial practices, spiritual performances, lifestyles, and other existential aspects cannot be ignored. To explain further, the spices that we use in our foods, the dresses that we wear, the cultures that we practice, the knowledge that we share, and the music that we listen to and/or perform, demonstrate varied forms of oceanic, and transoceanic links. The links can be located in terms of the sociohistorical, intergenerational, conflictual, and collaborative relationships that humans have been sharing with the oceans. These different oceanic and transoceanic perspectives about the societies and cultures around us show that oceans are not only aquatic entities, but also social, cultural, historical, emotional, esthetic, and familial entities that cannot be disentangled from our habitual thoughts and actions.

This book, through the creolized spiritual, culinary, and musical practices of the African diaspora in India and the Indian diaspora in South Africa, invites us to reinterpret the existing societies and cultures with and through the porous and fluid interconnectedness of the oceans. The sociocultural possibilities, dreams, resistance, and crises of the African Indians in India and South African Indians in South Africa, as discussed in this book, remind us that the mainstream neoliberal sociocultural practices have not been sufficiently interrogated and interrupted. Interrogations and interruptions are only possible when histories and cultures across societies are documented in meticulous, diverse, and unconditional ways. This book makes such an effort by discussing different transoceanic creolized cultural practices and the necessity of practicing them in contemporary times.

The uniqueness of this book lies in documenting various oral narratives that have otherwise remained restricted within the families and communities of African Indians and South African Indians to date. The oral narratives question the stereotypical ways in which many books and articles have presented these communities. However, the arguments in this book are inconclusive in nature and will continue to take place through diverse patterns and mediums in the future.

## Endnote

1 A town located in the Purba Medinipur district along the coast of Bay of Bengal.

## References

Wilson, R. S. 2022. 'Introduction: Worlding Asia Pacific into Oceania – Worlding Concepts, Tactics and Transfigurations against the Anthropocene'. In *Geo-Spatiality in Asian and Oceanic Literature and Culture*, edited by S.S. Chou, S. Kim and R.S. Wilson, 1–32. New York & London: Palgrave.

Hofmeyr, I. 2021. *Dockside Reading: Hydrocolonialism and the Custom House*. Johannesburg: Wits University Press.

Menon, D., Zaidi, N., Malhotra, S. and Jappie, S. 2022. *Ocean as Method: Thinking with the Maritime*. London & New York: Routledge.

# ACKNOWLEDGMENTS

This book is a result of multifarious transoceanic and transborder interactions with scholars and activists in India and South Africa at different moments of time and space. I would like to begin my exhaustive list of acknowledgment with Professor Melissa Steyn for kindly agreeing to host me as a Postdoctoral Fellow at the Wits Centre for Diversity, University of Witwatersrand for more than two years and thoroughly supporting me in developing this monograph as a part of my postdoctoral project. I would extend my gratefulness to Kudzaiishe Vanyoro and Michelle Mapimbiro for being a great family and introducing me to amazing Afro-Indian creole foods and food stories. I would like to acknowledge the time and energy that Jamie Martins dedicated to go through a few chapters of this book and suggest necessary revisions. I would appreciate Rapti Siriwardane-de Zoysa and Bhargabi Das for writing a powerful foreword and afterword respectively. Devarakshanam Govinden (popularly known as Aunt Betty) cannot be thanked enough for being so warm and motherly and consistently advising me in building my research. I would like to appreciate the delicious creole foods, food stories and hospitality of Sanza Sandile at the Yeoville Dinner Club, Johannesburg and of Stephne Du Rand and Danille Du Rand at their home in Pretoria. I would also like to extend my love to Rajendra Chetty for hosting me at his home, warmly preparing delicious foods for me and introducing me to diverse South African-Indian culinary cultures. Also, how can I forget the utter guidance, support, and encouragement of Professor Ananya Jahanara Kabir and Professor Ranjan Ghosh for their time, energy and effort to build my knowledge on transoceanic creole studies, ecology, and environment. It is also needless to say that without the conversations on food, culture, music, and spirituality with Ishay Govender, Bobby Marie, Kalim Rajab, Nissar Pangarkar, Chats Devroop, Dilip Menon, Suria Govender, Siddharthiya Pillay, Vasugi Singh Dewar, Parusha Naidoo, Rozena Maart, Omar Badshah, and Professor Lewis R. Gordon in South Africa and with Hameeda Makwa Siddi, Farooq Murima Siddi, Qayyum Murima Siddi, Farida Al-Mubrik, Soumali Roy, and

Rafiq Siddi in India, this project would have never developed. Last, but not the least, I would also like to extend my humble gratitude for the untiring technical support and guidance that I have received from Mario Rosair, Jebaslin Hephzibah and other members of the editorial and production team for shaping this project with so much love, warmth, and care.

# Chapter 1

# INTRODUCTION:
## *NOMOSHKAR-SANIBONA-VANAKKAM-MOLWENI-HUJAMBO…*

Are our identities fixed, or do they travel across races, communities, religions, societies, cultures, economies, geographies, cosmologies, epistemologies, and ontologies? This question is not new. Sociohistorically, this question has been asked and addressed from multiple geopolitical vantage points. But one should never stop asking this question. This question is a consistent reminder of our existential liminalities, fluidities, porosities, and ambiguities that we habitually perform through our thoughts and actions within diverse spatiotemporal contexts. I am initiating my book with this particular question because this question lies at the heart of the thematic and theoretical arguments of this book. As we travel across different states, countries, and continents, we are welcomed in different cultural spaces in different ways. The ways of greeting each other are often characterized by various similarities. The similarities are not mere coincidences but are underpinned by the ancestral histories and memories of social, cultural, political, and economic exchanges across different spaces and times. For instance, Lewis R. Gordon, a professor from the University of Connecticut, always begins his lectures by greeting the audience in Hindi, Hebrew, English, Tamil, Xhosa, and Zulu. This is not any form of "attractive gimmick" (Ngai 2020, p. 1), but a benevolent and sincere way of remembering his ancestral roots and remembering the routes through which his ancestors have traveled across cultures. Lewis believes that his process of scholarship building is interwoven with the constellations of ancestral knowledge that he has intergenerationally imbibed from his foremothers and forefathers, and it is necessary to acknowledge such multiple rootedness in shared academic and activist spaces through greetings.

Greetings perform powerful social, cultural, political, and esthetic roles in making us feel "welcomed" and "unwelcomed" within cultural frameworks. Whenever we meet strangers who greet us in our respective languages, we immediately feel emotionally and esthetically connected to them, irrespective of not knowing them. This is how greetings function as "conditions for social encounters" (Duranti 1997, p. 63). Now coming to thematic and the theoretical contexts of this book, on a similar note, the evolution of the African Diaspora in India and the Indian Diaspora in South Africa has been based on multiple levels of territorial, geographical, commercial, political, social, economic, and cultural encounters. Before progressing further, it is necessary to clarify the perspective in which the term "Diaspora" has been used in this book. With respect to the research contexts of this book, the term "Diaspora" has been used to refer to "a particular framing of a 'call of history' and a particular framework for cultural self-making that people respond to according to class position, alienating political events, and their local political imagination" (Hansen 2012, p. 17). Having said this, let us see how the African Diaspora and the Indian Diaspora communities have been sociohistorically shaped through multiple encounters.

Hasmukh Sankalia, in his book *The Prehistory of India* (1977), mentions that the presence of "First Punjab Man" has been located in the Kashmir regions of India and Pakistan with Acheulian tool kits and hand axes (1977, p. 38). The toolkits and hand axes date back to 2 million B.C. and are identical to the kits of the *Homo Erectus* that have been found in South, East, and North Africa. Besides Kashmir, the Acheulian tool kits have also been found in Andhra Pradesh and Karnataka, but the dates of origin could not be calculated (Baptiste 2008, p. 119). James Shrieve, in his book *The Neandertal Enigma* (1995), says that a DNA analysis by the Indian Statistical Institute on 30 different ethnic groups in India reveals that the "first populations in India arrived from Africa, then rapidly expanded and diversified" (p. 75). With the establishment of the New Kingdom in Egypt between the 16th and 11th centuries B.C., the trade exchanges between India and Africa got regularized and diversified. In the article "Indus-Euphrates-Nile" (1965), Kishore Kumar Saxena argues that during the regime of the New Kingdom India imported copper, gold, wood, and ivory from Egypt, while Egypt imported lapis lazuli and sandalwood from India (p. 201). According to Kishore, "by the second half 2nd millennium B.C., there is concrete evidence of a network of trade linking up the whole area from the Tigris to the Indus and the Oxus and its extension West of the Euphrates as far as the Nile. This traffic involved movement of goods and, side by side, of people" (1965, p. 202). Abu Minda Yimene in his article, "History of Indo-African Trade Relations and the Resulting Slave Trade" (2008), discusses that after the Islamic capital shifted from Syria to Iraq (in Baghdad) in 750 A.D., the Persian Gulf came close to the Indian Ocean through trade networks. As a result, on the one side, the trade networks between India and Africa expanded, and on the other side, the arrival of slaves to India (Gujarat, Karnataka, and Maharashtra)

**Figure 1:** The entrance to the coast of Kuda in Bhavnagar Gujarat, which, according to the Siddi folklores functioned as the gateway for the African traders and other traders from modern-day Iran, Iraq, and Syria.

also increased (Figure 1). The East African island towns functioned as an active market space for the Gujarati Muslims and the Arabs to indulge in the purchase and sale of African slaves (pp. 484–485).

The first Islamic invasion in Maharashtra and the Deccan took place in the 1300s, and they brought several Africans as slaves and mercenaries from the eastern parts of Africa. Pashington Obeng in his article "Religion and Empire" (2008), notes that "from the beginning of the Bahmani empire (1347–1489) in the Deccan, Africans (Habshis/Abyssinians) served as mercenaries (*jangju*) fighting for or against various political and military powers" (p. 236). Ibn Battuta, in his travelogues (written in the 14th century), notes that the Muslim rulers in India not only maintained a slave community of Africans (mostly East Africans) but also gave them away as gifts to the distinguished visitors. Ibn Battuta, who was a distinguished visitor in the court of the Sultanate of New Delhi, was "gifted a slave girl" (Baptiste 2008, p. 141). In the late 15th century, Bengal was ruled by an African kingdom (1487–1493), and the rulers arrived in the state from Ethiopia (Roychowdhury 2016). The African kingdom saw four kings within six years. Edward Alpers in his article, "Gujarat and the Trade of East Africa" (1976), notes that during the rule of Sultan Mahmud I and Sultan Mahmud II, Gujarat's commercial relations with East Africa diversified, and the import of African slaves and mercenaries increased (p. 32). Shanti Sadiq Ali, in his book *African Dispersal in the Deccan* (1996), talks about how the African slaves, mercenaries, and merchants regulated the domestic and interstate affairs of the states in the Deccan (pp. 34–37).

When William Hawkins and Sir Thomas Roe visited India between 1608 and 1619, they realized that several Abyssinians were a part of the population of "Indostan," apart from "Hindoos" and "Mohametans" (Foster 1926, p. 61). In 1672, Abbe Carre came to Gujarat through Syria, Iraq, and the Persian Gulf, and in his historical documents, Carre said that during the 17th century, India housed a large number of Africans who were part of a "wide array of occupations like kings, slaves, eunuchs, guards, etc." (Baptiste 2008, p. 150). Louis de Grandpre arrived in Pondicherry from the Maldives through the Malabar Coast and Ceylon. In his records, he mentioned the existence of black towns in Pondicherry, Madras, Deccan, and Calcutta (1814, p. 16). Paul E. Lovejoy's *Transformations in Slavery* (2012) records that in the 19th century, around 25,000 African slaves "were shipped north to Arabia, Persia, and India" (p. 152). In *The Last King of India* (2014), Rosie Llewellyn-Jones discusses the African men, women, and eunuchs that Wajid Ali Shah had in his kingdom in Lucknow in the 19th century (pp. 128, 134–137, 139, 141, 143, 171–172). Rosie also talks about a platoon of women soldiers, popularly known as the Gulabi Platoon, that fought against the British during the Sepoy Mutiny in 1857 (2014, p. 128). Every article and book that has been mentioned above elaborately reflects on how the repertoire of greetings played a crucial role in building the social, cultural, economic, and political exchanges between the Africans and the Indians in India (Haring 2007; Declich 2018; Sharpe 2020).

Similarly, when the Indians traveled to South Africa as slaves, indentured laborers, and merchants, different linguistic, verbal, and esthetic expressions of greetings functioned as crucial tools to develop sociocultural relations between the Indians and the native indigenous locals. When the Indians were brought as slaves and indentured laborers to South Africa by the British and Dutch, they were segregated from each other and kept with the local native slaves. The purpose behind practicing this segregation strategy was to prevent the slaves from communicating with each other and revolt against the colonial masters (Lovejoy 2012; Datta 2013; Alpers 2014). But communication was inevitable, and the process of greeting each other in their respective languages gave birth to creolized social, cultural, linguistic, and esthetic spaces, which have been elaborately discussed in the subsequent chapters. The museum archives of Kenya, Zanzibar, Mozambique, Ethiopia,

Tanzania, Uganda, South Africa, and other eastern and southern African nations consist of several paintings and photographs that show Indians from Gujarat and Maharashtra being greeted by the local natives on the eastern African coasts (Hopper 2011; Abungu 2014; Hawkes and Wynne-Jones 2015). The paintings depict how through different physical and facial expressions, the Africans greeted the Indians. These greetings multiplied into a variety of socioeconomic relations later.

The presence of Indians in the eastern parts of Africa dates back to the 11th century AD. Horton, in his book *Shanga* (1996), mentions finding bronze figures of lions in the stone town of Shanga, which is located on the northern coast of Kenya (p. 81). According to Horton, the figures date back to the 11th century. Archaeologists discovered golden figures of one-horned rhinoceros in Mapungubwe in South Africa, which are believed to have arrived with the Indian merchants in the 13th century (Oddy 1995, p. 186). During this time, a few Indian merchants started settling in different parts of eastern and southern Africa and this is how the Indian Diaspora in these parts of Africa evolved. Several historical records reveal that from the early 17th century, the Indians started traveling to different parts of eastern and southern Africa regularly as slaves, indentured laborers, and merchants (Gregory 1971; Alpers 1976; Oonk 2015). As the Dutch arrived on the Malabar Coast (in India) from Ceylon in the 16th century to take control of the spice trade, besides spices, they also started transporting Indian slaves from Bengal and Malabar to southern Africa (Datta 2013; Reddy 2016). Both Datta and Reddy in their respective works argue that around 70 percent of the foreign slaves in South Africa between the 17th and 19th centuries came from India. In the 19th century, several Indian businessmen traveled to Zanzibar, Tanzania, and Kenya, established commercial relations with the local merchants, and settled there (Oonk 2015). During the same time, the apartheid era widely contributed toward the development of the Indian Diaspora in South Africa, where Indians arrived as slaves, indentured laborers, merchants, and sociopolitical activists (Dickinson 2015, p. 80). Besides social, political, and economic exchanges between India and Africa, the exchange of sociocultural greetings between the Indians and the Africans in their respective languages historically generated collaborative, reciprocative, and creolized spaces for transcontinental and transoceanic knowledge production.

The title of this chapter is a synecdochic portrayal of how different linguistic and cultural patterns of greeting have been mobilizing the transcontinental and transoceanic sociocultural exchanges between India and southern Africa over different moments of time and space. Greetings as a phenomenal tool for regulating sociocultural exchanges between the African Diaspora in India and the Indian Diaspora in South Africa continue to function in the contemporary era. During my fieldwork with the South African Indians in Johannesburg, Pretoria, and Durban and the African Indians in Gujarat, the South African Indians greeted me in Hindi, Tamil, and Malayalam, and the African Indians greeted me in Swahili and Zulu. The greetings in diverse languages made me feel welcomed in the communities, helped me to comfortably interact with the community members, and allowed me to actively participate in their creolized cultural discourses. The outcome of the interactions will be elaborately outlined in the forthcoming chapters of this book.

Before proceeding further, let me clarify the social, cultural, and historical positionality that motivated me to weave this project. I was born in the city of Kolkata, India, and my familial origins, on the mother's side as well as on the father's side, lie in Faridpur and Dhaka in Bangladesh. During the Bangladesh Liberation War in 1971, my grandparents and parents were forced to migrate to what is known as West Bengal today. After arriving in West Bengal, they settled in the districts of Maldah and Raiganj. During my childhood days, I went to my ancestral homes in Maldah and Raiganj and went around visiting different historical monuments like palaces, forts, mosques, and temples that date back to the 13th century (Figure 2). While

**Figure 2:** This is the image of Hazrat Bilal Masjid. It was constructed in 1422 in the memory of Bilal Habshi from Ethiopia by the African merchants in Kuda, Gujarat.

visiting these places, my grandparents would narrate stories about the sociohistorical origin of these monuments, and it is from them that I came to know that there existed an African kingdom in Bengal in the 15th century. A few of their architectural remnants, like the Firuz Minar and the Choti Dargah, exist in Maldah today. The Firuz Minar was built by the second king of the African dynasty (also known as the Habshi dynasty), known as Saifuddin Firoz Shah[1] and the Choti Dargah (small shrine) is believed to have been constructed by Shams-ud-din Muzaffar Shah—the last king of the Habshi dynasty. When I orally came to know about this historical narrative, I wondered why we were not taught these histories in our schools? My grandparents also shared with me that how the family members and African slaves of the African kings married with the locals and settled in different parts of Bengal (Dey and Dey 1994).[2] Such marriage alliances have given birth to the interracial communities of the African Indians (or Afro-Indians) in Bengal.

Gradually, with time, through oral and written narratives, I came to know about the historical existence of various such African (and later African Indian) kingdoms in different parts of India like Telangana, Karnataka, Maharashtra, Gujarat, Goa, Kerala, and Daman and Diu. I also came to know about how the Indians traveled to different parts of southern and eastern Africa for varied social, cultural, political, and economic purposes and settled there. The sociohistorical narratives about the African Diaspora in India and the Indian Diaspora in South Africa are not discussed in the history syllabuses of the schools and higher education institutions in India and South Africa. A lot of the linguistic structures, food habits, fashion ethics, musical performances, spiritual practices, and dance patterns in India have historically been derived from the sociocultural practices of the African immigrants, and a lot of such sociocultural practices in South Africa have been derived from the Indian immigrants. This detailed clarification of my positionality is motivated by how "our identities predispose us to see or not see; listen to or not listen to; read or not read; cite or not cite; concern ourselves or not concern ourselves; with specific Other people, issues, and societal dynamics" (Moya 2011, p. 79). In the context of this aspect, I wish to acknowledge the fact that I am not an expert on the Indian Diaspora in South Africa and the African Diaspora in India. It is the interest in the history, culture, and contemporary existence of these communities that has driven me to develop this research. Being completely aware of my position as a community outsider, I wish to share that I collaborated with these communities for this project with the presumption that "*all* knowledge is situated knowledge: there is *no* transcendent subject with a 'God's Eye' view on the world who ascertains universal truths independent of a historically- and culturally-specific situation" (Moya 2011, p. 80). Therefore, every information and argument in this book has been shaped through personal conversations with these communities and by critically analyzing unpublished notes, documentaries, research articles, and books that engage with the history and culture of the African Diaspora in India and the Indian Diaspora in South Africa.

On the basis of my positionality, the research methods that I have used in this book and the way they have been implemented are as follows:

a. *Critical Diversity Studies*: This method ensures that research observations and arguments are not interpreted and reduced to a singular narrative framework. Melissa Steyn, in her article "Critical diversity literacy" (2015) observes that within the methodological framework of critical diversity studies, "differences of many varieties increasingly co-exist" (p. 379). The research works that have been conducted for this project take into account the multiple narratives about the sociohistorical origin and practices of the African Diaspora in Gujarat and the Indian Diaspora in South Africa, and the diverse spatiotemporal positionalities from where the narratives emerge. The book does not come to a singular conclusion but shares every possible narrative about the musical, culinary, and dance practices of the African Diaspora and the Indian Diaspora communities that have been collected in oral and written ways.

b. *Intersectionality*: Intersectionality as a research methodology unfolds how different forms of social, cultural, political, economic, and geographical practices are intertwined with each other and how they can never be assessed separately. The dance, musical, and culinary practices of the African Diaspora and the Indian Diaspora have been discussed in this book in an interwoven manner. To elaborate further, the book reflects on how the spiritual, culinary, and musical practices of the African Indians in India and the South African Indians in South Africa are socioculturally interrelated.

c. *Participatory Action Research and Guesthood*: While researching with communities, the methodologies of participatory action research and guesthood invite us to treat the community members not as passive data objects of research, but as active co-researchers. In the article "Guesthood as Ethical Decolonising Research Method" (2003), Graham Harvey observes that the methodology of guesthood is generated by the concern that "our methods, approaches, and outcomes are not only appropriately academic but are also both ethical and decolonising in the experience of those among or with whom we research" (p. 126). During my fieldwork with the South African Indians in South Africa and the African Indians in Gujarat, I firmly observed the ethical values of participatory action research and guesthood by asking them elaborative open-ended questions like: "Can you please share stories about your musical practices?"; "Can you please reflect on your habitual lifestyles?"; "Can you please talk about your food habits?"; "Can you please talk about your spiritual beliefs and practices"; etc. and by analyzing their sociocultural practices in the ways they were described by the community members. The community members also invited me to actively participate in their songs and dances as a part of their guesthood practices.

d. *Emvoicement*: Irma McClaurin in her book *Women of Belize* (1996) defines "emvoicement" as a research methodology that involves "a collective process of talking, documenting and writing about certain issues" (p. 12) without depending on prerecorded audios and videos. Emvoicement allows the researchers to document and interpret the narratives of the participants through lived experiences. Similar to participatory action and guesthood, emvoicement enables the participants to work as coresearchers, coactors, and coauthors. On a similar note, the Siddi participants in India and the Indian participants in South Africa have played an active role as coresearchers and coauthors of this book. Though I have solely put all the thoughts in the written form in this book, but every participant from India and South Africa have played an active role in shaping those thoughts. This methodological application gets thoroughly reflected in the participant narratives in the following chapters of this book.

e. *Thematic Network Analysis*: In this book, I have used Jennifer Attride-Stirling's framework of thematic network analysis. In the article "Thematic networks" (2001), Jennifer observes that "thematic analyses seek to unearth the themes salient in a text at different levels, and thematic networks aim to facilitate structuring and depiction of these themes" (p. 387). According to her framework, the thematic network is structured over three components: global theme, organizing theme, and basic theme. On the basis of this framework, the book has been widely divided into three overarching themes and they are spiritual practices, culinary practices, and the musical practices of the African Indians in India and the South African Indians in South Africa. Under each of these themes, different subthemes have been generated on the basis of the conversations with the research participants in India and South Africa.

Altogether, 11 research participants from South Africa (across Johannesburg, Pretoria, and Durban) and 4 research participants from India (Gujarat) were interviewed. The interviews were conducted in a semi-structured manner. The interviews with respect to the participants in South Africa were conducted both in-person and online, and the interviews with participants from India were conducted in-person. Based on interests and availabilities, the research participants were selected through the snowball sampling method. During the interviews, permissions were sought from the participants before using their original names in this book.

f.  *Kin Study*: The interviews that have been conducted with the community members are based on the method of "kin" studies and not "case" studies. To elaborate further, instead of treating the community members as mere information givers and data providers, kin studies invite us to "engage more thoughtfully and reciprocally with land [and water], non-human beings, and people…" (Rubis 2020, p. 816). In a similar way, the conversations with the participants and the theoretical arguments that have emerged out of them, engage with the narratives of the human beings on the one side, and the narratives of the nonhuman beings like the Indian Ocean, ships, spices, seeds, musical instruments, and culinary objects on the other. Being an Indian from India, the method of kin study also allowed me to closely observe the various sociocultural similarities and dissimilarities between the Indian communities in India and the South African Indians in South Africa, and between the African Diaspora in India and the native indigenous African communities in South Africa. Apart from conducting semi-structured interviews, I have participated in community lunches at different Hindu temples in Durban and in different religious rituals like the fire-walking festival[3] at Sithambaram Alayam Temple and the *Navratri* festival[4] at Luxmi Narayan Temple in Chatsworth.

g.  *Citing Community Members*: Usually, personal communications with community members are presented as footnotes or endnotes, or in a separate unpublished section at the end of articles/chapters. Such a citation approach not only reduces the participants as mere objects of data collection but also ignores their active role in the research. To acknowledge the role of the African Indian and the South African Indian community members as coresearchers, I have used the citation template that has been conceptualized by Lorisia MacLeod in her article "More than Personal Communication" (2021). She has developed this template to cite the voices of the "indigenous elders" and the "knowledge keepers" (Macleod 2021) from the indigenous communities.

The Diasporic communities across the Indian Ocean, like the South African Indians in South Africa and the African Indians in India (in the context of this book), have transformed the oceanic space into a region. In the article "Mobile communities of the Indian Ocean" (2020), Khatija Khader observes: "Diasporic identities enable understandings of the role and significance of territory in the (re)creation of identities as these identities are experienced as globalized or non-localized and are not necessarily restricted by spatial affliations" (2017, p. 77). In order to clarify her arguments, Khatija further adds: "This does not imply that spatial affiliations like nation-states are not primary identification for most individuals, but rather, it stresses that identity is and has been experienced in multiple ways that are not necessarily, spatially restricting—that is as regional, trans-regional and universal" (p. 77). The musical, culinary, and the spiritual practices of the African Indians in Gujarat and the South African Indians in South Africa, which would be elaborately reflected in the following chapters, are multi-rooted across the Indian Ocean both in India and South Africa, and cannot be restricted within specific geopolitical compartments. As a result, both these communities occupy complex identity spaces in their respective countries, within which they have to consistently juggle between multiple forms of identities—social, cultural, racial, official, political, national, geographical, and others.

Based on these arguments, the book has been divided into six chapters. The introductory chapter titled "Introduction: *Nomoshkar-Sanibona-Vanakkam-Molweni-Hujambo…*"[5] sets the pace of this book by discussing how different repertoires of greetings have sociohistorically contributed toward shaping the transcontinental and transoceanic exchanges between India and South Africa. The chapter also reflects on my theoretical and methodological positionality, and what motivated me to curate this book project.

Chapter 2, titled "Porosity: Reservations and Fluidities," discusses how the Indian Diaspora in South Africa and the African Diaspora in India occupy complex and "in-between" spaces of caste, class, religion, politics, and economy. The chapter has been composed based on the fieldwork that has been conducted in Gujarat in India and Durban in South Africa. The fieldwork consists of audio recordings, video recordings, and interviews.

Chapter 3 is titled "Spiritual Memories," and it unpacks the different spiritual memories that the African Indians in Gujarat and the South African Indians in South Africa engage with on a habitual basis to keep their ancestral roots alive. While outlining the various spiritual memories, the chapter also argues how the spiritual mnemonic practices of these communities within their respective geopolitical spaces are creolized in nature. The arguments in this chapter have been supported by the viewpoints of the research participants from Gujarat and Durban, who have shared their reflections on the spiritual practices that they observe and how they have sociohistorically inherited the practices.

Chapter 4, titled "Musical and Dance Memories" reflects on the diverse forms of musical and dance cultures that are practiced by the African Indians and the South African Indians. Their musical practices, on the one side, uphold their respective ancestral roots, and on the other side, they have woven diverse creolized performative patterns in the forms of musical instruments, orchestra, and dance. The creolized musical performances of the Indian Diaspora and the African Diaspora have been discussed in this chapter through existing research works and field research. The chapter also discusses how musical performances influence the sociocultural existential state of these communities in the contemporary era.

Chapter 5, titled "Culinary Memories," engages with the diverse culinary practices of the African Indian community in Gujarat and the South African Indians in South Africa. Besides certain native indigenous African food habits, the African Indians uphold a creolized food culture in India. On the other side, in South Africa, the Indian Diaspora has diversely contributed toward generating Indian and creolized food cultures in the country.

Chapter 6, titled "Continuity: Weaving Archipelagoes of Resistance," summarizes the findings of this book and argues how the discussions on creolized spiritual, culinary, and musical practices of the African Indians in Gujarat and the South African Indians in South Africa disentangle the historical narratives of these communities from the colonially structured epistemological and ontological enclaves of knowledge production and generate archipelagos of intersectional knowledge spaces. The chapter also discusses how this book functions as an archive of creolized memories for present and future research projects that focus/are going to focus on the Indian Ocean World Diaspora in general and these communities in particular.

## Endnotes

1  Prior to becoming a king, Saifuddin Firoz Shah was a eunuch slave and his slave name was Malik Andil Habshi.
2  The oral narrative has been cited on the basis of the citation template as shared by Lorisia MacLeod, an indigenous member of the James Smith Cree Nation, in her article titled "More Than Personal Communication." Link: https://kula.uvic.ca/index.php/kula/article/view/135/258. More details about the relevance and the context of this citation methodology can be found in the "Research Methodologies" section of this chapter.
3  The fire-walking festival is mostly observed by the low-caste Hindus in South Africa in honor of Goddess Gangaiammen (an incarnation of Goddess Luxmi). Goddess Gangaiammen is regarded as the goddess of spiritual and material wealth. In Durban, it is usually performed in two temples—Gangaiammen Temple and Sithambara Alayam Temple. In the Sithambara Alayam Temple, it is organized on the last Sunday of July every year. A medium-sized square-shaped walking area is constructed with mud, cement and sand. Burning pieces of firewood are placed in the walking area and the devotees take their turns to walk bare feet over the firewood. The process of walking is often complemented with the experiences of spirit possession.
4  The word "nav" means nine and "ratri" means nights. *Navaratri* is a Hindu religious festival, which is annually organized for nine nights for the worship of Goddess Durga (responsible for combating demons and social evils).

5   The Bengali word for "hello" is "nomoshkar," the Zulu word for "hello" is "sanibona," the Tamil word for "hello" is "vanakkam," the Xhosa word for "hello" is "molweni," and the Swahili (also often said by the Siddis in Gujarat as a greeting) word for "hello" is "Hujambo."

# References

Abungu, G.H.O. 2014. 'East Africa: Museums'. In *Encyclopedia of Global Archaeology*, edited by C. Smith, 2273–2281. New York: Springer.

Ali, S.S. 1996. *The African Dispersal in the Deccan: From Medieval to the Modern Times*. New Delhi: Orient Longman.

Alpers, E.A. 1976. 'Gujarat and the Trade of East Africa, c. 1500–1800'. *The International Journal of African Historical Studies* 9, no. 1: 22–44.

Alpers, E.A. 2014. *The Indian Ocean in World History*. Oxford: Oxford University Press.

Attride-Stirling, J. 2001. 'Thematic Networks: An Analytic Tool for Qualitative Research'. *Qualitative Research* 1, no. 3: 385–405.

Baptiste, F.A. 2008. 'From "Invisibility" to "Visibility": Africans in India through the Lens of Some Select Sources from the Late Classical Period to the Late 18th century A.D'. In *TADIA: The African Diaspora in India*, edited by K.K. Prasad and J-P. Angenot, 117–166. Bangalore: Jana Jagrati Prakashana.

Datta, A. 2013. *From Bengal to the Cape: Bengali Slaves in South Africa from 17th to 19th century*. Sydney: Xlibris Corporation.

Declich, F. 2018. 'Translocal Relations Across the Indian Ocean An Introduction'. In *Translocal Relations Across the Indian Ocean*, edited by F. Declich, 1–48. Leiden: Brill.

Dey, J. and Dey, P.K. Lived in Maldah. 'Oral Teaching. History of Africans in Bengal'. June 21, 1994.

Dickinson, J. 2015. 'Articulating an Indian Diaspora in South Africa: The Consulate General of India, Diaspora Associations and Practices of Collaboration'. *Geoforum* 61: 79–89.

Duranti, A. 1997. 'Universal and Culture-Specific Properties of Greetings'. *Journal of Linguistic Anthropology* 7, no. 1: 63–97.

Foster, William. 1926. *The Embassy of Sir Thomas Roe to the Court of Great Mogul, 1615–1619, as Narrated in His Journal and Correspondence*. London: Oxford University Press.

Gregory, R.G. 1971. *India and East Africa: A History of Race Relations within the British Empire, 1890–1939*. Oxford: The Clarendon Press.

Hansen, T.B. 2012. *Melancholia of Freedom: Social Life in an Indian Township in South Africa*. Princeton: Princeton University Press.

Haring, L. 2007. *Stars and Keys: Folktales and Creolization in the Indian Ocean*. Indiana: Indiana University Press.

Harvey, G. 2003. 'Guesthood as Ethical Decolonising Research Method'. *Numen* 50, no. 2: 125–146.

Hawkes, J.D. and Wynne-Jones, S. 2015. 'India in Africa: Trade Goods and Connections of the Late First Millennium'. *Afriques* 6, https://doi.org/10.4000/afriques.1752.

Hopper, M.S. 2011. 'East Africa and the End of the Indian Ocean Slave Trade'. *Journal of African Development* 13, no. 1–2: 39–66.

Horton, M.C. 1996. *Shanga: The Archaeology of a Muslim Trading Community on the East Coast of Africa*. London & Nairobi: British Institute in Eastern Africa.

Khader, K. 2017. 'Mobile Communities of the Indian Ocean: A Brief Study of Siddi and Hadrami Diaspora in Hyderabad City, India'. In *Global Africans: Race, Ethnicity and Shifting Identities*, edited by T. Falola and C. Hoyer, 76–93. New York: Routledge.

Llewellyn-Jones, R. 2014. *The Last King of India: Wajid Ali Shah*. New Delhi: Penguin Viking.

Lovejoy, P.E. 2012. *Transformations in Slavery: A History of Slavery in Africa*. New York: Cambridge University Press.

Macleod, L. 2021. 'More Than Personal Communication: Templates for Citing Indigenous Elders and Knowledge Keepers'. *KULA: Knowledge Creation, Dissemination and Preservation Studies* 5, no. 1, https://doi.org/10.18357/kula.135.

McClaurin, I. 1996. *Women of Belize: Gender and Change in Central America*. New Brunswick. NJ: Rutgers University Press.

Moya, P.M.L. 2011. 'Who We Are and From Where We Speak'. *Transmodernity: Journal of Peripheral Cultural Production of the Luso-Hispanic World* 1, no. 2: 79–94.

Ngai, S. 2020. *Theory of the Gimmick: Aesthetic Judgment and Capitalist Form*. Cambridge and London: The Belknap Press of Harvard University Press.

Obeng, P. 2008. 'Religion and Empire: Belief and Identity among African Indians of Karnataka, South India'. In *India in Africa, Africa in India*, edited by J.C. Hawley, 231–252. Bloomington: Indiana University Press.

Oddy, A. 1995. 'Gold Foil, Strip, and Wire in the Iron Age of southern Africa'. In *Ancient & Historical Metals: Conservation and Scientific Research*, edited by D.A. Scott, J. Podany and B.B. Considine, 183–196. Los Angeles: The Getty Conservation Institute.

Oonk, G. 2015. 'India and Indian Diaspora in East Africa: Past Experiences and Future Challenges'. *ODI: Organisation for Diaspora Initiatives*. 15 November. http://www.odi.in/recent-conferences/interactive-lecture-on-india-and-indian-diaspora-in-east-africa-past-experiences-and-future-challenges-by-dr-gijsbert-oonk-erasmus-university-holland-2-december-2015-at-conf-hall-2-at-iic/.

Reddy, E.S. 2016. 'Indian Slaves in South Africa: A Little-Known Aspect of Indian-South African Relations'. *South African History Online*. 8 January. https://www.sahistory.org.za/archive/indian-slaves-south-africa-little-known-aspect-indian-south-african-relations-e-s-reddy.

Roychowdhury, A. 2016. 'African Rulers of India: That Part of Our History We Choose to Forget'. *The Indian Express*. 27 May. https://indianexpress.com/article/research/african-rulers-of-india-that-part-of-our-history-we-choose-to-forget/.

Rubis, J.M. 2020. 'The Orang Utan Is Not an Indigenous Name: Knowing and Naming the Maias as a Decolonizing Epistemology'. *Cultural Studies* 34, no. 5: 811–830.

Sankalia, H.D. 1977. *The Prehistory of India*. New Delhi: Munshiram Manohar Pvt. Ltd.

Saxena, K.K. 1965. 'Indus-Euphrates-Nile'. *Indo-Asian Culture* XIV: 200–204.

Sharpe, J. 2020. *Immaterial Archives: An Africa Diaspora Poetics of Loss*. Illinois: Northwestern University Press.

Shrieve, J. 1995. *The Neandertal Enigma: Solving the Mystery of Modern Human Origins*. New York: Penguin Viking.

Steyn, M. 2015. 'Critical Diversity Literacy: Essentials for the 21st Century'. In *Routledge International Handbook of Diversity Studies*, edited by S. Vertovec, 379–389. New York: Routledge.

Yimene, A.M. 2008. 'History of Indo-African Trade Relations and the Resulting Slave Trade'. In *TADIA: The African Diaspora in India*, edited by K.K. Prasad and J-P. Angenot, 483–496. Bangalore: Jana Jagrati Prakashana.

# Chapter 2

# POROSITY: RESERVATIONS AND FLUIDITIES

The transcontinental and transoceanic exchanges of people and cultures between India and the continent of Africa got regularized with the arrival of the European colonizers. Before the arrival of the Portuguese in India, the movement of Africans to India was not regular and was not restricted to slavery (Toninato and Cohen 2010). As discussed in Chapter 1, Africans with diverse professional affiliations arrived in India with diverse professional intentions. On May 20, 1498, when Vasco da Gama reached the coast of Calicut from the East African coastal town of Malindi, he was received by "two North African merchants from Tunis who reportedly spoke both Spanish and Italian" (Alpers 2014, p. 68). This encounter between Christopher Columbus and the Africans shows the professional and linguistic diversity that the African immigrants had in India before the arrival of the European colonizers. It was with the arrival of the Portuguese colonizers in India that the African slaves in India were racially dehumanized and compartmentalized. As the Portuguese came to India, they brought with them African slaves from Mozambique, Eritrea, Somalia, and South Africa, which diversified the already existing population of Abyssinian slaves in the country (Shah et al. 2011; India Today Web Desk 2016; Vallangi 2016). The Portuguese subjected the African slaves to severe states of existential inhumanity, as they did with the indigenous communities in other parts of the world. As a result, many slaves escaped from the clutches of the Portuguese into the forests of Goa, Maharashtra, Karnataka, and Gujarat. This is how the African settlements in Gujarat came into existence.

The sociocultural diversity of the African Indians in India can be traced back to the different names by which they are known. Historically, the African Indians in India were known as Siddis and Habshis. Several narratives revolve around the origin of the term "Habshi" and "Siddi." According to Fitzroy Baptiste, the term "Habshi" can be traced from the ancient Egyptian word "Khebtsi," which was used to refer to the people of Punt (ancient Ethiopia) (Baptiste 2008, p. 121). Sergew Sellassie, in her book

*Ancient and Medieval Ethiopian History upto 1270* (1972), mentions that ancient Ethiopia was also referred to as "Neter" by the ancient Egyptians, which means the "the land of the Gods" (p. 21). Many historians claim that the "Habshis" were referred to those Africans who came to India from Ethiopia. Wilfred H. Schoff argues that the ancient Egyptian inscriptions have used the word "Hbsti" to denote the people from Punt (Schoff 1995, p. 62). Based on these different perspectives, Baptiste observes that the Amharic (the native language of Ethiopia) root for the word Ethiopia is "Itiopyavan," which in turn has been derived from the word "atyob," meaning "incense." So, the meaning of the word "Habshi" can be translated as "gatherers of incense" (2008, p. 121). Schoff also noted that the root for the word "Hbsti" lies in the Arabic word "Habash" or "Habashat," meaning the "people of Abyssinia or Ethiopia" (1995, p. 63).

British historian John Burton-Page has a different narrative to share about the origin and usage of the term "Habshi." In his third edition of the *Encyclopedia of Islam* (1971), Burton-Page says: "The majority, at least in the earlier periods, may well have been Abyssinian, but certainly the name was applied indiscriminately to all Africans, and in the days of the Portuguese slave-trade with India, many such "Habshis" were in fact of the Nilotic and the Bantu races" (pp. 14–15). With respect to the term "Siddi," there are not many perceptions about its origin. According to the 9th edition of the *Oxford English Dictionary* (1933), the term "Siddi" originated from the Arabic word "Sayyid," meaning "lord" or "prince" (p. 22) (Figures 3 and 4). Robert Vane Russell, in his book *The Tribes and Castes of Central Provinces in India* (2015), reflects that "Siddi" is commonly used to denote the Africans (either Abyssinian or Negro) in India (p. 145). Baptiste observes that in *Bhagavadgomandal*, an encyclopedia that was compiled under the patronage of Maharaja Bhagvatsinhji of Gondal in the early 20th century, the term "Siddi" is equated with "Habshi" and "Negro" (p. 122). Reginald Enthoven, in his book *The Tribes and Castes of Bombay* (1990), argues the same (p. 332).

Besides diverse geographical and cultural origins, the diverse etymological origins of the African Indians in India have led to the development of what Ananya Jahanara Kabir and Ari Gautier identify as archipelagic memories and fragments (2021). Similar to a group of islands, the cultural performances of the African Indians distinctly display the diverse social, cultural, geographical, and historical aspects of India and eastern Africa within their archipelagic sociocultural spaces. These spaces are porous and fluid, where the cultural performances of the African Indian community do not get restricted within specific geopolitical enclaves and move back and forth in multiple directions like liquid entities. Radhika Seshan, in the "Afterword" to the book *Indian Ocean Histories*

**Figure 3:** A shrine of Baba Gor in the Bedi district of Jamnagar.

identifies the phenomenon of porosity as an "amphibian approach," where sociohistorical narratives "move from land to water and back again" (2020, p. 264). Ananya Jahanara Kabir, in one of her lectures, further elaborates on the phenomenon of porosity by comparing porosity with a "semi-permeable membrane that allows matters to pass in both directions" (2021a). In the same

**Figure 4:** Juma Masjid in Ahmedabad. The meticulous architectural work was created by Siddi Abbas. Siddi Abbas was an African guard in the palace of Ahmad Shah Badshah.

lecture, she also adds that porous cultural performances "allow a two-way flow" (2021a). The instances of porous cultural performances by the African Indian communities in Gujarat, as discussed in the following chapters, show that their sociocultural practices flow in multiple directions through lands, littorals, and oceans at the same time.

But the porous and fluid sociocultural practices of these communities have been consistently interrupted by racial discrimination in the contemporary era. The African Indian communities in Gujarat and other parts of India are racially discriminated against in terms of caste, class, economy, skin color, and geography. Though the African Indians in Gujarat geographically exist across different cities and forests, they are physically and ideologically confined within enclaves. The enclaves have been architecturally, racially, culturally, and economically constituted in a marginalized, demonized, and dehumanized manner by the other communities. The African Indians in Gujarat experience multiple forms of infrastructural crises, like a lack of access to basic health facilities, educational facilities, communication facilities, and job facilities in their localities. The local governing bodies have not taken any initiative to improve the infrastructural conditions of the African-Indian residential areas in Gujarat. On the contrary, every effort is being made by the governing organizations and the private enterprises to uproot these communities from their respective lands and confiscate their lands for industrial purposes (Sansad TV 2017). Besides geographical racialization, the community is also racialized in terms of their religion and skin color. While traveling in trains and buses and at their workplaces, they are often ridiculed because of their hairstyles and dark skin colors (101 India 2016; Stuart 2018). Despite sufficient skills, many offices in Gujarat refuse to recruit African Indians because they are often perceived as foreigners (AFP 2021; Asthana 2021). Within the socioreligious systems in India, the Hindu African Indians are regarded as low castes, the Muslim African Indians are regarded as low-class Muslims, and the Christian African Indians are perceived as inauthentic Christians (Czekalska and Kuczkiewicz-Fras 2016).

These diverse racial experiences have pushed the African Indians within a liminal diasporic existential framework, where they live "on the threshold of society, enduring a life of segregation and oppression, marked by difference underscored by mourning for lost homelands, in the everyday practices of living" (Gairola et al. 2021, p. 5). In the article "Liminal Diasporas in the era of Covid-19," Rahul Gairola, Sarah Courtis, and Tim Flanagan understand liminal Diasporas as "subjective bodies in motion that are dangerously marked by difference, otherness, alterity, and precarity" (2021, pp. 4–5). The African Indians in Gujarat exist "neither here nor there" and they are "betwixt and between the positions assigned and arrayed by law, custom, convention and ceremonial" (Turner 1969, p. 95). Technically, the African Indians in Gujarat are regarded as the tribal communities of India, and they have been granted the status of Scheduled Tribes.[1] But personal conversations with the African Indians in different parts of Gujarat have revealed that despite being granted reservations and scholarships at government-run education and work institutions, due to racial biases, a majority of the African Indians work as domestic workers, cleaners, untrained laborers, agricultural workers, garage mechanics, tourist guides, and in other odd jobs (Community Members 2019a).

The porous and fluid sociocultural practices and the liminal diasporic experiences can be located among the South African Indians in South Africa as well. The Indian Diaspora in South Africa centrally originated with the transoceanic transportation of slaves by the European colonizers. Markus Vink, in his article "The World's Oldest Trade," mentions that between 1626 and 1662, the Dutch exported slaves mostly from the "Arakan-Bengal coast" and a few from the Malabar coast to the Cape with "reasonable regularity" (2003, p. 142). Besides transporting slaves directly from India, Indian slaves were also transported by the Dutch from Batavia[2] (Prakash 1985, p. 149). Nigel Worden in his book *Slavery in Dutch South Africa* (1985), reveals that besides the Dutch, the British also brought a considerable number of slaves from India to the Cape in the first half of the 18th century (p. 48). Besides Cape, South Africa received more than "150,000 Indians, most as indentured workers on the sugar cane plantations of Natal, while a better educated class of so-called passenger Indians because they purchased their own passage also journeyed to Durban from the 1870s" (Alpers 2014, p. 118). A majority of the Indian slaves who were either directly transported from India or through Batavia to the Cape in South Africa were proselytized as Christians. In fact, many Indian slaves who came through Batavia have already socioculturally cross-pollinated with the local Malay residents of Batavia. Therefore, when the Indian slaves arrived in South Africa, they brought creolized sociocultural practices along with them, which were visible through their spiritual, culinary, and musical performances. After interacting and cross-pollinating with the local native communities in South Africa, the creolized sociocultural spaces of the Indians got further diversified and reciprocative. During my fieldwork in Durban, I came across several South African Indian families who continue to acknowledge the creolized sociocultural patterns that they have imbibed from their parents and grandparents in an unassimilated manner. The foods that they consume, the dresses that they wear, and the music that they listen to and perform reflect their awareness of their Indian ancestral roots on the one side and their acknowledgment of the local native cultures and traditions of South Africa on the other. Sociohisorically, this is how, the creolized sociocultural practices of the African Indians in India and the South African Indians in South Africa have unpacked a "permanent state of becoming: folding, shifting, arching, twisting; always in motion" (Gordillo quoted in Bremner 2015, p. 9). These practices of "co-becoming in a relational world" (Country 2016, p. 460) have been elaborately discussed in the consequent chapters.

But the processes of practicing the porous and fluid cultural traditions have been sociohistorically punctuated with the racialization, marginalization, and criminalization of the South African Indians, for which the South African Indians themselves are widely responsible. A majority of the passenger Indians, who came as merchants and traders to South Africa, did not want to socially, culturally, and racially identify themselves at par with the local black communities. With the arrival of the passenger Indians, internal sociocultural hierarchies between the passenger Indians and the indentured Indians were also visible. Thomas Hansen observes that "caste was not reproduced in the same forms as in India, but caste consciousness remained strong" (p. 74). The caste consciousness has been maintained in terms of religious, linguistic, and ritualistic affiliations. Thus, in Chapter 3, I have specifically reflected on the spiritual practices of the Indian indentured labor communities in South Africa. Thomas also adds that "the interest in purified Hinduism, India, and cultural authenticity has become central to the performance of respectability within the middle class among South African Indians" in the contemporary era (p. 203).

Many Indian merchants and traders collaborated with the Dutch, British, and Afrikaans to evict the local native communities from their ancestral lands and occupy them. Even many Indian slaves, due to their commitment and sincerity, were promoted as assistants, housekeepers, and cooks in European households. Later on, when the practice of slavery was officially disbanded in South Africa, many Indian slaves gained complete or a portion of their properties as gifts from the colonial masters. The Indians used these properties to establish agricultural farms and businesses and recruited local black natives as helpers. The local black natives were not treated any differently from the slaves by the Indians. During the preapartheid and the Apartheid eras, they always wanted to maintain their racial distinctiveness by indulging more in commercial activities and avoiding menial jobs. During the apartheid era, the Indians played a crucial role in fighting against colonial violence, but the protest movements were underpinned by racial segregation. Several historical records reveal that Indian political activists during Apartheid were more focused on liberating their fellow Indians and South Asians from the clutches of the colonial rule, and less interested in the sufferings of the local black natives of South Africa (Jain 1999; Ebr.-Vally 2001; Vahed et al. 2010; Desai and Vahed 2016). Many Indians took part in the anti-apartheid struggles to meet their self-centric desires of gaining leadership in the government.

Such racially and culturally hierarchical attitudes get reflected through the mistreatment of black domestic workers and Indians (whose family has originated from the indentured labor communities)[3] at workplaces and homes; a tendency to mostly engage in white-collar jobs; a reluctance to get identified as South Africans; and the maintenance of a high-caste distinctive Indian identity that is attached to a "deep and affective sense" of South Asian Hindu cultural practices (Hansen, p. 17). To elaborate further, today, the practices of racial segregation and hierarchies against the black communities and treating the black existential spaces as hunting and gathering grounds for capitalistic profits can be found through the preference of white staffs and fair-skinned high-caste Indian staffs over black staffs and low-caste dark-skinned Indian staffs in many Indian marriages, the exploitation of local wealth for commercial profits, the systemic practices of political corruption, and in many other ways (Rhodes Archive 2013; Buccus 2020; Bagchi 2021). During personal conversations, the South African Indian participants in Durban revealed that due to a certain group of racially violent elitist and casteist South African Indians, the rest have to suffer from racial abuse from the local black communities. The outbreak of the Phoenix Massacre in the surrounding areas of KwaZulu-Natal on July 8, 2021, is a recent and appropriate example. During the massacre, the local Black South Africans destroyed many shops that were run by the South African Indians and in return, the South African Indians unleashed physical violence on the local blacks, leading to several deaths (Eligon and Mji 2021; Erasmus and Hlangu 2021). Before the Phoenix Massacre, several other acts of anti-Indian violence, like the Durban riots in 1949, the attacks against Indians by the Zulu people in Durban in 1985, and many others, had taken place in South Africa.

These complex experiences of the African Indians in Gujarat and the South African Indians in South Africa have been triggered by what Gabeba Baderoon philosophizes as "perilous intimacies" (2014, p. 52). The perilous intimacies or harmful intimacies between the European colonial masters on the one hand and the African servants in India and the Indian servants in South Africa on the other hand, were commonly experienced by the servants, kitchen workers, cooks, and mine workers. As servants, kitchen workers, cooks, and mine workers, the Africans and the Indians were compelled to work closely with the colonizers, irrespective of their disinterest. Later on, when slavery and indentured laborship were abolished, the Africans in India and the Indians in South Africa did not have any other option but to settle in India and South Africa, respectively, and socially, culturally, politically, economically, and emotionally intermingle with the local communities. As already discussed above, the process of intermingling has been fraught with sociopolitical conflicts and tensions.

To overcome the sociopolitical conflicts and tensions and to establish collaborative, co-creative, nondiscriminatory, affectionate, and creolized spaces of existence with the local communities, the South African Indians in South Africa and the African Indians in India use their porous and fluid sociocultural practices as tools of performing their ancestral memories on the one side and weaving archipelagic archives of peacebuilding, reciprocity, togetherness, and diversity on the other. As discussed in the following chapters, the creolized sociocultural practices of these communities have given birth to the phenomenon of what Kuan-Hsing Chen in *Asia as Method* (2010) identifies as "critical syncretism" (p. 101). Chen understands critical syncretism as a cultural practice that can "generate a system of multiple reference points" (2010, p. 101). The multiple reference points have the capability to "break away from the self-reproducing neocolonial framework that structures the trajectories and flow of desire" (Chen 2010, p. 101). The following chapters challenge the neocolonial frameworks of historical knowledge production about the Indian Ocean World by discussing how the performances of ancestral memories in a creolized manner have been sociohistorically empowering the South African Indians and the African Indians to gradually convert their experiences of perilous intimacies into secured intimacies. Chapter 3 engages with their creolized spiritual practices.

## Endnotes

1   The term "Scheduled Tribes" (STs) was first used in the Constitution of India under Article 366(5). Scheduled Tribes refer to native indigenous community groups, who have originated in India or have originated somewhere else and have been settled in India for a considerable period of time. The status of Scheduled Tribes grants scholarships and reservations at educational and job institutions to the native indigenous communities.
2   Batavia was a colony of the Dutch East Indies, and it corresponds to present-day Jakarta in Indonesia.
3   The Indians who have originated from the indentured labor communities can be identified through their names and surnames.

## References

101 India. 2016, June 2. *Siddis: In It for the Long Run – Unique Stories from India* [Video file]. YouTube. https://youtu.be/ped-uIlw_24.
AFP. 2021. 'African Tribe, Long Marginalised in India, Seeks Sporting Glory'. *Al Jazeera*. Accessed 9 December 2021 at: https://www.aljazeera.com/sports/2021/3/31/african-tribe-long-marginalised-in-india-seeks-sporting-glory.
Alpers, E.A. 2014. *The Indian Ocean in World History*. Oxford: Oxford University Press.
Asthana, D. 2021. 'The Siddi: An African Tribe's Story of Slavery, Racial Oppression and Hope in India'. *Ariana*. 9 December. https://www.arianalife.com/topics/community/discrimination/the-siddi-an-african-tribes-story-of-slavery-racial-oppression-and-hope-in-india/.
Baderoon, G. 2014. *Regarding Muslims: From Slavery to Post-apartheid*. Johannesburg: Wits University Press.
Bagchi, S. 2021. 'How Crony Capitalism of a Few Indians Led to Fatal Anger in South Africa'. *The Wire*. 24 July. https://thewire.in/world/gupta-brothers-south-africa-india-kwazulu-natal-zuma.
Baptiste, F.A. 2008. 'From "Invisibility" to "Visibility": Africans in India through the Lens of Some Select Sources from the Late Classical Period to the Late 18th century A.D'. In *TADIA: The African Diaspora in India*, edited by K.K. Prasad and J-P. Angenot, 117–66. Bangalore: Jana Jagrati Prakashana.
Bremner, L. 2015. 'Fluid Ontologies in the Search for MH370'. *Journal of the Indian Ocean Region* 11, no. 1: 8–29.
Buccus, I. 2020. 'Racism by and against Indian South Africans Poisons Our Land'. *Daily Maverick*. 27 July. https://www.dailymaverick.co.za/opinionista/2020-11-27-racism-by-and-against-indian-south-africans-poisons-our-land/.

Burton-Page, J. 1971. *Encyclopedia of Islam*. Leiden: Brill.

Chen, K-H. 2010. *Asia as Method: Toward Deimperialization*. Durham and London: Duke University Press.

Community Members. Lives in Ahmedabad. Oral Conversation. 2019a. 'Existential Conditions of African Indians in Gujarat'. 14 April.

Country, B. 2016. 'Co-becoming Bawaka: Towards a Relational Understanding of Place/Space'. *Progress in Human Geography* 40, no. 4: 455–475.

Czekalska, R. and Kuczkiewicz-Fras, A. 2016. 'From Africans in India to African Indians'. *Politeja* no. 42: 189–212.

Desai, A. and Vahed, G. 2016. *The South African Gandhi: Stretch-Bearer of Empire*. Stanford: Stanford University Press.

Ebr.-Vally, R. 2001. *Kala Pani: Caste and Colour in South Africa*. Cape Town: Kwela Books.

Eligon, J. and Mji, Z. 2021. 'Indian vs. Black: Vigilante Killings Upend a South African Town'. *The New York Times*. 4 September. https://www.nytimes.com/2021/09/04/world/africa/South-Africa-Phoenix-riots-deaths.html.

Enthoven, R.E. 1990. *The Tribes and Castes of Bombay*. Bombay: Asian Educational Services.

Erasmus, D. and Hlangu, L. 2021. ' "Phoenix Massacre": What Really Happened in the Deadly Collision of Brutalised Communities'. *Daily Maverick*. 28 July. https://www.dailymaverick.co.za/article/2021-07-28-phoenix-massacre-what-really-happened-in-the-deadly-collision-of-brutalised-communities/.

Gairola, R.K., Courtis, S. and Flanagan, T. 2021. 'Liminal Diasporas in the Era if COVID-19'. *Journal of Postcolonial Writing* 57, no. 1: 4–12.

India Today Web Desk. 2016. 'Meet the Siddis: India's Very Own African Community'. *India Today*. 11 June. https://www.indiatoday.in/fyi/story/siddi-community-in-india-indian-africans-south-africa-13632-2016-06-11.

Jain, P.C. 1999. *Indians in South Africa: Political Economy of Race Relations*. New Delhi: Kalinga Publishers.

Kabir, A.J. 2021a, October 27. *Creole Indians: Porosity as Necessity* [Video file]. YouTube. https://youtu.be/ySBcJObIERU.

Kabir, A.J. and Gautier, A. 2021, January 22. *The archipelago of fragments and Creole Indias: 'South Asia' on le thinnai kreyol* [Video file]. YouTube. https://youtu.be/ILIFIanuvq8.

Prakash, O. 1985. *The Dutch East India Company and the Economy of Bengal, 1630–1720*. Princeton: Princeton University Press.

Rhodes Archive. 2013. 'The Guptas and Racism among Indian People'. *Rhodes Archive*. 15 May. https://www.ru.ac.za/perspective/2013archive/theguptasandracismamongindianpeople.html.

Russell, R.V. 2015. *The Tribes and Castes of the Central Provinces of India*. Scotts Valley: CreateSpace Independent Publishing Platform.

Sansad TV. 2017, May 20. *RSTV Documentary – Siddis of Karnataka* [Video file]. YouTube. https://www.youtube.com/watch?v=WqgNnqb7_Z8&t=943s.

Schoff, W.H. 1995. *The Periplus of the Erythraean Sea: Travel and Trade in the Indian Ocean by a Merchant of the First Century*. New Delhi: Munshiram Manoharlal Publishers Pvt. Ltd.

Sellassie, S. 1972. *Ancient and Medieval Ethiopian History to 1270*. Addis Ababa: United Printers.

Seshan, R. 2020. 'Afterword'. In *Indian Ocean Histories: The Many Worlds of Michael Naylor Pearson*, edited by R. Mukherjee and R. Seshan, 264–268. London & New York: Routledge.

Shah, A.M. et al. 2011. 'Indian Siddis: African Descendants with Indian Admixture'. *American Journal of Human Genetics* 89, no. 1: 154–161.

Stuart, A. 2018, April 22. *Inside a Lost African Tribe Still Living in India Today* [Video file]. YouTube. https://youtu.be/B_a1WS5ncDk.

Toninato, P. and Cohen, R. 2010. 'The Creolization Debate: Analysing Mixed Identities and Cultures'. In *The Creolization Reader: Studies in Mixed Identities and Culture*, edited by P. Tominato and R. Cohen, 1–22. London & New York: Routledge.

Turner, V. 1969. *The Ritual Process: Structure and Anti-Structure*. London & New York: Routledge.

Vahed, G., Desai, A. and Waetjen, T. 2010. *Many Lives: 150 Years of Being Indians in South Africa*. Pietermaritzburg: Shuter and Shooter Publishers.

Vallangi, N. 2016. 'India's Forgotten African Tribe'. *BBC*. 5 August. https://www.bbc.com/travel/article/20160801-indias-forgotten-jungle-dwellers.

Vink, M. 2003. 'The World's Oldest Trade: Dutch Slavery and Slave Trade in the Indian Ocean in the Seventeenth Century'. *Journal of World History* 14, no. 2: 131–177.

Worden, N. 1985. *Slavery in Dutch South Africa*: Cambridge: Cambridge University Press.

# Chapter 3

# SPIRITUAL MEMORIES

## Introduction: Spiritual Relationalities of the Ocean

The history of the creolized spiritual practices of the African Diaspora in India and the Indian Diaspora in South Africa unpacks complex narratives of "sacredscapes" (Jeychandran 2019, p. 17) that emerged around the Indian Ocean littorals during the movements of the slaves and indentured laborers. Makrand Mehta in "Gujarat Sufis, "Sants," and the Indian Ocean World in Medieval Times" (2019) observes that "along with the exchange of commodities, information, and ideas, knowledge was also shared" (p. 163). The movements of the indentured Indian laborers to South Africa and the African slaves to India gave birth to "multiple worldings in an emergent world of many worlds" (Uimonen and Masimbi 2021, p. 35) through the development of porous and fluid creolized spiritual practices in their respective geographical spaces in the forms of coastal shrines and transoceanic worship cultures. The creolization is specifically visible in terms of the emergence of transoceanic and interreligious folklores; the preparation of creole foods as offerings to gods, goddesses, and devotees; the usage of Afro-Indian creole languages in religious songs; and the usage of multicultural worship procedures.

It is also important to note that with respect to the creolized spiritual practices of the Indian Diaspora in South Africa, this chapter has exclusively focused on the spiritual practices of the Indian indentured laborers because the Hindus who came as passenger Indians mostly from Gujarat and Uttar Pradesh rejected any forms of transcultural influence on Hinduism, adhered to high caste puritan religious practices, and did not regard the indentured Indians as "genuine" Hindus because of their tendency to interweave Hindu spiritual practices with local African and other spiritual practices. The economically flourishing situation of the Hindu passenger Indians enabled them to bring in Brahmin priests from India (Kumar 2012; Lal and Vahed 2013). The Brahmin priests were brought from India because they were "informed largely by the Sanskrit ritual texts" (Kumar 2012, p. 392) and could assist the high-caste Hindu passenger Indians to re-establish their puritan Hindu practices in South Africa. Such an adherence to high-caste puritan Hindu religious practices has led to the foundation of organizations like, South African Hindu Mahasabha and the Hindi Shiksha Sangh. The former organization promotes the practice of "pure" Hinduism, which is a metaphor for high-caste Hinduism, and the latter organization promotes the Hindi language and North Indian Hindu culture for the Hindus in South Africa (Meer 1969, pp. 209–210).

Bill Freund captures the internal spiritual and caste hierarchies among the Hindus in South Africa in a more meticulous way in the book *Insiders and Outsiders: The Indian Working Class of Durban 1910–1990* (1995). He says:

> Temples and shrines dotted the landscape. Rambling homesteads were fitted for domestic shrines appropriate to memorials and sacrifices. Rituals which focused on specific divine incarnations, typical of village India, arrived early. After 1900, visiting scholars brought more philosophical and reformed versions of Hindu belief, particularly to those of north-Indian origin with claims to a higher caste background. The Barracks (and no doubt peripheral areas, one of which is still famous for its fire-walking ceremonial) witnessed a variety of Hindu ritual performances, Tamil religious dramas and six-foot dances. These were activities that were seen and participated in by the whole community, men and women. (p. 37)

The different forms of ritualistic practices among the different castes and classes were systematized through the establishment of separate communal organizations like the Young Men's Vedic Society (1905) and the Hindu Tamil Institute (1914) by the Tamils, the Andhra Maha Sabha (1931) and the Pathmajuranni Andhra Sabha (1933) by the Telugus, the Arya Yuvuk Sabha (1912) by the Hindus from Calcutta (who were mostly Hindi-speaking people), and the Natal Rajput Association (1911) by the Rajput community from northern and western India (Henning 1993).

On the other side, with respect to the discussions on the creolized spiritual practices of the Siddis in Gujarat, this chapter has specifically focused on the Siddi community of Ahmedabad, Jamnagar, and Bhavnagar,[1] who trace their origin from the slaves, and not on the Siddis, who trace their origin from the Siddi royal household of Sachin.[2] Many Siddis who claim their origin from the royal households do not regard the Siddis who originated from African slaves as "original" Siddis. This claim is logically very problematic and is a way to maintain racial and class hierarchies. The following section focuses on the various creolized spiritual practices of the Indian indentured

Hindus in South Africa and how the practices have been functioning as a tool of sociocultural empowerment for them.

## From Crises to Creolization

The creolized spiritual practices of the Indian indentured laborers in South Africa can be located through the intermingling of traditional Hindu spiritual practices with Muslim, Christian, and local African spiritual practices. When the indentured laborers (mostly low-caste Hindus and a few high-caste Hindus) boarded the ships from India to come to Natal in South Africa, the caste and class divisions collapsed. On the ships, irrespective of different castes and religions, all the Indians were expected to eat together and eat the same food that was cooked in the same pot (Devroop 2022). But, with the passage of time, as the arrival of the indentured laborers and later on the passenger Indians in South Africa increased, the caste-based divisions among the Hindu Indians in South Africa started brewing up. Especially with the arrival of the passenger Indians, the presence of the high-caste Hindus gradually increased in South Africa. In order to maintain their cultural rootedness in India, the high-caste Hindus started building caste-based sociocultural compartments in South Africa. The differences were generated in terms of the spiritual Puritanism that existed in India with respect to skin color, food habits, knowledge about Hindu rituals, and castes. During a personal conversation, Chats Devroop from Durban, who traces his family lineage from a male indentured laborer (his uncle) of Bihar and currently works in the Department of Music at the University of Pretoria, shared how the high-caste Hindus believed that the indentured laborers did not know how to worship the Hindu gods in an authentic and ethical manner. Chats also added: "The indentured laborers had the capability to adapt to the local scenario. For example, during the Hindu rituals in North India, usually the leaves of wood apple trees are used. But, due to lack of wood apple trees in Natal and Durban, we have been using banana leaves at home to perform the rituals" (2022). Chats' description shows how creolized forms of spiritual practices were developed by the indentured Hindus through using local plants during religious rituals.

Besides Chats Devroop reflecting on the capability of the indentured Indians to adapt locally, Omar Badshah, a spiritual leader, social activist, and archivist for South African History Online (SAHO), who traces his family lineage from the village of Dwarka, a town in Gujarat, shared how the Hindu indentured Indians actively participated in Islamic religious practices. He talked about the participation of the indentured Hindus in Muslim religious festivals like Muharram in Durban. The festival of

Muharram in Durban is popularly known as "Coolie Christmas" because from the late 19th century to the early 20th century, this was the only festival which the indentured Indians and the local African slaves could publicly celebrate. During a conversation, Omar Badshah noted that "from the later part of the 19th century to the early part of the 20th century, most Hindus celebrated Muharram" (2022). He also added that, along with the Muslims, many Hindus regularly offer prayers at the cemetery of Badshah Pir (a Muslim spiritual leader) in Durban. In this way, this festival has historically functioned as a cultural melting pot for many indentured Indians and local Africans in Durban. Even today, many Hindus actively participate in the Muharram processions through singing, dancing, and carrying *Tazias*[3] along with the Muslims.

The interreligious creolized practices of the indentured Hindus, as highlighted by Omar, also get reflected in the observations of Ravi Govender, the spiritual head of the Sithambar Alayam (previously known as the Old Umbilo Temple). The temple is located in the Bayview area of Chatsworth. Ravi's parents were Dalits[4] and they came to Natal from Madras (presently known as Chennai) around the 1940s as indentured laborers in the sugarcane plantations. Along with various other indentured Hindus, they led to the foundation of the Old Umbilo Temple in 1960. During the conversation, Ravi shared that the temple acknowledges religious diversity through worshipping Hindu deities like Sithamman,[5] Durga,[6] Shiva,[7] and various others on the one hand and Jesus Christ on the other. The Hindu idols, instead of being garlanded with flowers, are garlanded with lemons.[8] Such a practice is similar to the usage of lemons in Zulu spiritual practices. During marriages and various traditional religious rituals, the Zulus wear girdles of flowers and lemons around their waist because they regard lemons as a spiritual symbol of life and purity. The adaptation of Zulu spiritual practices within Hindu spiritual practices by the indentured Hindus in South Africa is quite usual because, socio-historically, since the arrival of the indentured Indians to the coast of Natal in South Africa, they have been closely associated with the Zulus through working together in the indentured farms, working together as personal servants in the colonial households, living in the same residential areas before the imposition of group area acts, and establishing businesses together. Besides the intercultural spiritual practices, the aspect of creolization can also be located in terms of the foods that are offered to the deities and devotees in the Sithambar Alayam.

The foods are an interesting combination of local African cuisines with Indian cuisines. For instance, as Ravi Govender mentioned, during various festivals, the deities and the devotees are often offered Samp, Sambar,

Madumbi curry, Breyani, and various forms of sweets (Govender 2022). Samp is a local African food widely consumed by the Zulu and the Bantu communities in South Africa and is made of maize. Usually, the Africans prepare Samp by soaking husked maize in the water. After the husked maize softens, it is removed from the water and is consumed with beans curry, beef curry, and various other curries. The indentured Indians have creolized the preparation of Samp through adding a variety of local Indian spices, like coriander powder, chili powder, turmeric, and various others. Such a creolized version of Samp is often served with Sambar[9] to the deities and devotees. Along with Samp and Sambar, the temple also serves Madumbi curry and Breyani. Madumbi is a type of yam and is grown locally in South Africa. Usually, the local African communities in South Africa consume Madumbi in the boiled form and in a saucy curry. The indentured Indians have creolized the cooking pattern of Madumbi by adding curry leaves, coriander powder, cumin powder, chili powder, and various traditional Indian spices along with local sauces. The Madumbi curry is often served with Breyani, which is a creolized vegetarian version of the standard Biryani. Unlike the standard Biryani, which is prepared in a hot and spicy way with spices like cinnamon, cardamom, red chilis, saffron, ghee, cloves, and various other spices, the Breyani is prepared in a mildly spicy way with lentils and local South African vegetables like zucchini, carrot, beetroot, peas, and yam and with a slight usage of coriander and cumin powders. The creolized culinary practices of the indentured Indian community in South Africa have been discussed in detail in Chapter 5.

Apart from mixing traditional Indian spices with local South African spices and vegetables, using local plants in Hindu spiritual worships, and building interreligious exchanges, spiritual creolization is also visible through the rituals of spirit possession and fire-walking. At different points of time in a year, the rituals of spirit possession and fire-walking are performed by the indentured Hindus across South Africa. During my research visits to Shree Gengaiamman Temple[10] and Sithambar Alayam in Durban, the spiritual heads of the respective temples shared that the rituals of fire-walking and spirit possession of the indentured Hindus in South Africa are identical to the fire-walking and spirit possession rituals of the Zulus, Bantus, and various other indigenous communities across Africa in general and South Africa in particular. The acts of spirit possession and fire-walking are mostly performed by middle-aged and old-aged Indian women. The ritual of fire-walking takes place over burning charcoal and wood that are spread across a designated area near the temples. According to the spiritual folklore of the indentured Hindus, it is only the individuals who are honest and spiritually dedicated can participate in fire-walking and spirit possession. Anyone trying to perform such spiritual activities may get injured. It is also crucial to highlight that the performances of fire-walking and spirit possession by the indentured Hindu women function as weapons of resistance against the patriarchally dominated Hindu religious cultures.[11] The practices of spirit possession and fire-walking is common among the Siddis in Gujarat as well, and they have inherited them from their eastern African ancestors and spiritual leaders. The following section elaborately focuses on these and various other forms of creolized spiritual practices of the Siddis in Gujarat.

The creolized spiritual practices have enabled the Indians to carve out a collaborative existential space of their own amidst the local blacks and the settler whites in South Africa. The spiritual practices function as a "never-ending process of cultural encounter and rebirth" and lead to the evolution of "multiplicity of cultures" (Breteque 2021, p. 2), thus allowing the indentured Indians and the local Africans to establish and interweave collaborative existential spaces in South Africa that are multi-rooted across various Indian Ocean littorals.

## Creolized Spiritual Practices by the Siddis in Gujarat

The Indian Ocean World Space brought "African spiritual practices to the shores of Gujarat" (Shroff 2019, p. 205). A majority of the African Indian community in Gujarat evolved from eastern and northeastern Africa, and their spiritual practices center on Bava Gor, Baba Habash, and Mai Misra. According to the Siddi spiritual folklores, Bava Gor, Baba Habash, and Mai Misra are siblings, and they arrived along with four other siblings to the coast of Kuda[12] in Gujarat around the 14th century from Abyssinia[13] through the Nubian Valley[14] (Hameeda Makwa Siddi 2022). The creolized spiritual practices of the Siddis can be identified through the usage of Swahili Creole words in the religious songs, the combination of indigenous African rituals and the Sufi Islamic rituals of India, and interreligious spiritual practices.

Before engaging further with the contemporary creolized spiritual practices of the Siddis in Gujarat, let us briefly reflect on how their creolized spiritual cults evolved. As narrated by Helene Basu in the chapter "Narratives of Transcendental Decision-Making" (2019), Saint Bava Gor was an Ethiopian (Abyssinian) military leader, who was sent from Mecca across the Indian Ocean to liberate the people from oppressive evil powers. As the saint reached the destination, he realized that the evil power was a demoness. This realization put Bava Gor in a state of dilemma because on the one side he was expected to kill the evil power, and on the other side he cannot use physical prowess against a woman because attacking women by men is strictly prohibited in Islam. Therefore, in order to navigate through this challenge, he proposed the demoness to play a board game with him. This board game would allow the world to make a choice between good and evil, "by avoiding physical contact" (Basu 2019, p. 193). As the game began, the demoness started using "trickery and sorcery (black magic), which delayed and deferred the conclusion of a decision determining a winner and a loser" (Basu, p. 193). In order to take control of the situation, Bava Gor's sister Mai Misra, appeared in the scene and physically confronted the demoness. During the confrontation the demoness was pushed "into the ground" (Basu, p. 194). However, the act of segregating the good and the evil remained incomplete, and this incompleteness is spiritually regarded as "ongoing uncertainty" (p. 194). The spirit possession practices and the worshipping procedures of Bava Gor, Baba Habash, and Mai Misra by the Siddis in Gujarat reflect complex spiritual entanglements and uncertainties, as reflected in the abovementioned story.

To elaborate further, similar to the indentured Hindus in South Africa, the practices of spirit possession and fire-walking that are performed by the Siddis in Gujarat are specifically carried out by the experienced Siddi community members, who have undergone spiritual training from the community elders since their childhood days. The spirit possessors have the capability to exist in the physical as well as the metaphysical realms. During a conversation, Hameeda Makwa Siddi, an elderly Siddi woman and an experienced fire-walker and spirit possessor (Figure 5), revealed that when the rituals of spirit possession are not taking place, at that time the possessors lead a "life of good and evil" like anybody else (2022). At the time of spirit possession, the possessors get physically and psychologically transgressed into the realm of metaphysics. Despite people being able to see the physical expressions and movements, Hameeda shared that after the possessors get possessed, they do not remember anything about their physical movements and what goes around them (2022). They feel like they have gone to sleep, and their sleep is often punctuated by dreams of confusing and haunting images. The possessors also believe that the images are a representation of the spirits from the metaphysical world, and they try to communicate with the possessors in a silent way. This complex experience allows the possessors to simultaneously exist in the physical and metaphysical spaces, and embrace a spiritual state of ongoing uncertainty. The ritual of spiritual possession has been imbibed by the Siddis of Gujarat from their African ancestors, and it enables them to remain connected to their spiritual roots. Besides rituals of spirit possession, the Siddis also perform fire-walking during Urs.[15] The fire-walking ritual is mostly performed by the Siddi women inside the dargahs.[16]

**Figure 5:** Hameeda Makwa Siddi. One of the oldest surviving Siddi woman in Gujarat.

Along with preserving the spiritual traditions of the ancestors, their alignment with Saint Bava Gor also functioned as an "important catalyst of change" and forged "new bonds of brotherhood" by reconstructing their identities from ex-slaves to fakirs[17] (Shroff, p. 209). Today, the songs, prayers, and stories of Bava Gor have enabled the African Indians of Gujarat to claim their lineage with this Abyssinian saint, "erase memories of slavery and anchor their identity into a new genealogy" (p. 210).

The spiritual healing rituals of the African Indians of Gujarat are interwoven with the local Sufi practices, which, in turn, have been inherited from "numerous travelers from the Middle East who spread their message in Gujarat" and founded many followers there (p. 164). For instance, the Sufi traditions of *tariquat* (path) and *balka* (induction) have been "creatively incorporated into the *fakir* tradition" by the African Indians (Shroff, p. 212). Both the fakir tradition of the African Indians in Gujarat and the Sufi tradition of the other Muslims of Gujarat are followed by drinking a sacred sweet potion from the same cup as that drank by the murshid (spiritual teacher). The saliva of the murshid is regarded as spiritually pious, and its transmission into the bodies of the worshippers signifies the "transmission of the spiritual legacy" (p. 212). The initiation and induction ceremonies are followed by the performance of *Dhamal*[18] (Figure 6) by the worshippers at the shrine, where they sing songs to Bava Gor, Baba Habash, and Mai Misra. The songs, popularly known as zikrs,[19] are sung in the Hindi, Gujarati, and Urdu. Such songs are often punctuated with Swahili Creole words (Figure 7).

**Figure 6:** A glimpse of Baithaaki Dhamaal in Jamnagar.

**Figure 7:** A glimpse of Dancing Dhamaal in Jamnagar.

Let us interpret a few zikrs that consist of Swahili Creole words. The zikrs were documented by Hameeda Makwa Siddi, Farooq Murima Siddi, Soumali Roy, and me. The zikrs are:

**I**
La illaha ililla Dhamama
Bol Navey
Chamka Dhamama Dhamama
Bol Navey
Bol Nubi Nubi Nubi Nubi
Habshi Mastana Dhamama
Bol Navey
Jungle ke Raja Dhamama
Bol Navey
Wo Habshi Diwana Dhamama
Bol Navey
Fir sab log boltey hain
Ya Navey bol Navey
Asra piroka asra humara
Bol Navey

Meaning: This zikr is in the Urdu, Hindi, and Swahili languages. The Swahili Creole words that have been used are *Dhamama* (a percussion instrument widely played within the communities in eastern Africa) and *Habshi* (referred to the Siddis who are of Abyssinian/Ethiopian descent). This zikr is usually sung as an expression of respect and reverence toward Allah. The zikr means that in the praise of Allah, it is not only the human beings who are signing "La illaha ililla," but the forests, birds, oceans, and musical instruments are also singing in a chorus. Besides singing praises for Allah, the *Dhamama* also sings praise for Habshi Mastana (a Siddi saint) and every other Siddi *pirs* (a Muslim spiritual guide).

## II

Ya bolo sabaya hua wey
Ya bolo sabaya hua wey
Hu sabaya
Salwale Nabi Sultan

Meaning: This zikr is sung in praise of Habshi/Siddi spiritual leader Nabi Sultan, who is believed to have first arrived in Gujarat on the coast of Kuda from the Nubian Valley. The zikr means that after praising Allah and Bava Gor, it is time to praise Nabi Sultan (another spiritual leader of the Siddis). The Swahili Creole words that have been used are *hu* (a common Swahili expression to give consent) and *sabaya* (means "it is ok/everything is alright"). The zikr means that if the blessings of Siddi Nabi Sultan exist, then no evil can befall on the Siddis of Gujarat.

## III

Saalmini Saalmini
Saalmini Miskini
Saalmini ya Malungo
Saalmini Saalmini
Saalmini Miskini
Saalmini ya Malungo
Haaji lele Haaji lele
Allah Allah Haaji lele
Haaji lele ya Malungo
Haaji lele Haaji lele
Allah Allah Haaji lele
Seem Mama Seem Dungo
Allah Allah Seem Dungo
Seem Mama ya Malungo

Meaning: In this zikr, the Swahili Creole words that have been used are *saalmini* (means "hello to all"), *miskini* (means "poor"), *Malungo* (referred to the one-string instrument called Malunga), *Seem* (a term referred to the people of Swahili origin), and *Dungo* (means "to come"). In this zikr, a poor girl is singing with a Malunga and sharing that her mother is sick. But she will not beg and does not want to receive any donation for the treatment of her mother. She will earn money through singing and playing Malunga for her mother's treatment. She also believes that her honest ways of earning will allow her to seek blessings from Allah. Though she and her mother are Swahili and they have come from the faraway lands of eastern Africa. Allah will keep blessing them as long as she keeps singing the name of Allah and play Malunga.

### IV
Kanga ye Kanga
Kanga Misri me wa
Kanga janni me wa

Meaning: In this zikr, the Swahili Creole words that have been used are *Kanga* (a small funnel-shaped musical instrument which consists of small stones and is played by shaking in different rhythms) and *me wa* (means "the release of sounds"). This zikr means that the *Kanga* is being played in such a spiritually esthetic way that it invokes the healing spirit and blessings of Mai Misra.

### V
Seemley Seemley Seemley
Seemley le Seem Paya
Seemley le Seem Paya

Meaning: In this zikr, the Swahili Creole words are *Seemley* (means "belonging to the Swahili people") and *Seem*. This zikr is a celebration of the blessings of Bava Gor and Mai Misra as received by the Siddis of Swahili origin across generations.

### VI
Ya le Ya le Ya le
Bareka
Dom Gori Badshah Bareka
Sidi ka dekho Tamasha

Meaning: In this zikr, the Swahili Creole expression that has been used is *Ya le* and it is a way of showing respect toward community elders. This zikr talks about how Siddi spiritual leaders like Bava Gor and Mai Misra blesses the Siddi community elders and how the blessings are received through songs and dance.

## VII
Allahamidulillah Gori Badshah
Ho ya hey
Kasi dey

Meaning: In this zikr, the Swahili Creole word that has been is *kasi* and it means doing/performing something in speedy manner and the Swahili Creole expression that has been used is *Ho ya hey* and it is a way of calling people. This zikr, talks about how the celebration of the life and teachings of Siddi saint Gori Badshah is celebrated through music and dance that are often performed in a loud, speedy, and frenzied ways.

## VIII
Gori Shah ka hey ye Goma
Gori Shah ka hey ye Goma
Gori Shah ka hey ye Goma
Jam tiri tiri
Jam tiri tiri
Jam tiri tiri
Ye Habas Khan ka Goma
Ye Habas Khan ka Goma
Ye Habas Khan ka Goma
Jam tiri
Jam tiri
Jam tiri
Ye Misr ka hain ye Goma
Ye Misr ka hain ye Goma
Ye Misr ka hain ye Goma
Jam tiri
Jam tiri
Jam tiri

Meaning: In this zikr, the Swahili Creole words that have been used are *Goma* [name of a form of musical performance where one-sided hand drums (also known as *Goma*) are played and songs are sung. This musical practice is widely prevalent across different parts of eastern, northeastern, and southern Africa and *tiri* (means "brightness"). In this zikr, praises are being sung in the memories of Siddi Gori Shah, Siddi Baba Habas Khan, and Siddi Mai Misra (all spiritual leaders of the Siddi community). The zikr says that the moment praises are sung in the names of these spiritual leaders, the world brightens up with light and energy.

It is crucial to clarify here that the Swahili words that have been used in the abovementioned zikrs are not identical to standard Swahili words. Though the first generation of Siddis in Gujarat could converse in the standard Swahili language, with the passage of time, the Swahili language got mixed up with Gujarati, Kathiawadi, and other local languages of Gujarat, and eventually gave birth to Swahili Creole. So, the Swahili words that are found in the following zikrs are creolized forms of standard Swahili. The meaning of the Swahili Creole words in the abovementioned zikrs has been interpreted in consultation with various Siddi community members in the cities of Ahmedabad, Bhavnagar, and Jamnagar. The interpretations are not the ultimate ones, and they keep varying across the different Siddi communities in Gujarat on the basis of their respective spiritual and geographical contexts.

Apart from linguistic creolization and the intermingling of indigenous African spiritual practices and the Sufi Islamic practices of India, the creolized spiritual practices of the Siddis in Gujarat can also be located through their interreligious practices. The interreligious practices among the Siddis in Gujarat have centrally evolved over the following folklore narratives:

a. *Running away of Goddess Luxmi from the kingdom of Ahmad Shah Badshah*: As narrated by Farooq Murima Siddi, once goddess Luxmi[20] gets annoyed with the unnecessary financial extravagance and inequalities in the kingdom of Ahmad Shah Badshah, and decides to leave the kingdom. As she is about to leave, Siddi Suzaad, an African guard, spots her near the "Teen Darwaza" (three gates)[21] (Figure 8) and enquires the reason behind her departure. She says that she is very disappointed with the state of economic discrepancies in the kingdom, and therefore she wishes to stay no more. Siddi Suzaad requests her not to leave, but she remains adamant. Then, Siddi Suzaad asks her if she could wait for some time and allow Siddi Suzaad to at least inform the king about her departure. Luxmi accepts this proposal and says that she would wait till Suzaad returns, and once he returns, Luxmi will take Suzaad along with her. Suzaad accepts the proposal and goes to the king.

Listening to the entire story, Ahmad Shah Badshah gets worried and suggests Suzaad to take a decision. Suzaad suggests that if Ahmad Shah can kill Suzaad, then Luxmi will remain in the kingdom because she assured that she won't leave without Suzaad. Ahmad Shah rejects this proposal by arguing that without any reason, he cannot kill Suzaad. So,

**Figure 8:** Teen Darwaza. One of the many entrances to the kingdom of Ahmad Shah Badshah and the core residential area of the Siddis in Ahmedabad.

Suzaad kills himself by cutting his throat, and in this way, Luxmi remains in the kingdom. But she gives one blessing and one curse to the Siddis. The blessing is that the Siddis will never face any form of financial crisis, and the curse is that they will never be able to accumulate wealth (Farooq Murima Siddi 2022). Today, many Siddis, especially those who are professionally associated with trade and commerce, regard Luxmi as their goddess of wealth and worship her.

    The presence of Hindu spiritual characters, Muslim characters, and African characters in the Siddi folklore can also be found in the case of the folklore that centers on the interaction between Mai Misra and Makhaan Devi.

b.  *The curse of Makhaan Devi*: As narrated by Qayyum Murima Siddi, Mai Misra, along with his seven brothers, arrived on the coast of Kuda in Gujarat. They arrived in the evening, and so they decided to take a rest and spend the rest of the evening in Kuda. While Mai Misra was taking rest, the seven brothers were taking a stroll along the seaside. As the seven brothers were strolling, one of the brothers was taken captive by Makhaan Devi.[22] When the brothers requested that Makhaan Devi to release him, she denied and said that she would keep him as her playmate. Disappointed, the seven brothers returned and informed Mai Misra about the incident. Mai Misra walked to Makhan Devi and requested her to release her brother. But Makhan Devi remained adamant. Then Mai Misra came up with an alternate proposal. She said that if Makhan Devi releases her brother, then Mai Misra will give her company, and they will bless and heal their devotees together (Qayyum Murima Siddi 2022). This is why Mai Misra and Makhaan Devi's coastal shrines face each other in Kuda. Also, among all the siblings, it is only Mai Misra's shrines that are always located in the coastal regions of Gujarat.

During *Urs* in Bhavnagar, the Siddis first perform *Dhamaal* at Makhaan Devi's temple and then goes to Mai Misra and Bava Gor's shrines to perform. During the spirit possession and healing rituals, an experienced and elderly Siddi woman invites the spirit of Makhaan Devi from the coast of Kuda to the dargah of Bava Gor and performs spirit possession rituals. In case the prayers are fulfilled, the Siddis offer cooked fish to Makhaan Devi, and then it is brought to the shrine of Bava Gor.

These interreligious folklores enable the Siddis to combine the local spiritual practices of offering fish, offering garlands to Makhaan Devi, and worshipping goddess Luxmi with the indigenous African spiritual practices of performing *Dhamals*, spirit possession, and healing.

## Creolized Spiritual Practices as Tools of Epistemic Freedom

The creolized spiritual practices of the indentured Indian Diaspora in South Africa and the African Diaspora in India have led to the emergence of knowledge networks of "ritual sites" across India and South Africa that are "embedded in land-based histories and mobilities" (Basu 2019, p. 190). The knowledge networks in turn have led to the formation of various "hybrid identities" (de Silva 2016, p. 12) through which these communities have maintained their respective ancestral spiritual traditions on the one hand and acknowledged the local spiritual traditions on the other. The combination of ancestral spiritual traditions and the local spiritual traditions have empowered these communities to counter the various forms of racial, cultural, spiritual, and religious marginalization that they have been sociohistorically experiencing in their respective geopolitical spaces.

Historically, the European colonizers and the various local communities regarded these Diaspora communities as subhuman communities "with no knowledge" (Ndlovu-Gatsheni 2020, p. 17). Their creolized spiritual practices have given birth to multidirectional sociohistorical networks of "ocean epistemologies" (Hofmeyr 2020, p. 44) and have opened up "different ways of being with others, relating, and dwelling in and across" the interconnected ocean world between India and South Africa (Wilson 2022, p. 5). The transoceanic interconnectedness helps these communities to weave possibilities of epistemic freedom through not imprisoning their knowledge systems within definite spiritual enclaves that are operated by the mainstream religious ideologies of Christianity, Islam, Hinduism, and other religions; creating global consciousness of their spiritual practices through public performances of zikrs and *Dhamals* and building online archives of their performances in the forms of Facebook pages, YouTube channels, etc.; generating historical, cultural and spiritual consciousness among the community members by performing zikrs, *Dhamals*, fire-walking, and spirit possession as in the case of the Siddi community and by performing fire-walking, spirit possession, Afro-Indian culinary cultures and Afro-Indian worshipping patterns as in the case of the indentured Indian community; and preserving the spiritual traditions of their ancestors by celebrating the birth and death anniversaries of spiritual leaders, gods and goddesses. Such initiatives have enabled these communities to maintain their distinct cultural voices and identities, resist every form of cultural assimilation, and open up (both physically and virtually) their cultural spaces to other communities.

The practices of these communities are also "a source of healing technologies," which has gained social, cultural, and spiritual prominence in different parts of South Africa and India through crossing the Indian Ocean waters (Hofmeyr, p. 44). The creolized practices have given birth to various forms of creolized sacredscapes across the Indian Ocean littorals in Gujarat and South Africa and have created "parallel set of geographies and temporalities imbued with spiritual possession" (Baderoon 2014, p. 81). The spiritual histories and cultures of the Siddis and the South African Indians may not be directly linked to each other, but the different similarities in their spiritual practices show that "each and every identity is extended through a relationship with the Other" (Glissant 1997, p. 11).

The rhizomatic relationship between the South African Indians in South Africa and the Siddis in Gujarat is further discussed through creolized musical practices in Chapter 4.

## Endnotes

1  Ahmedabad, Jamnagar, and Bhavnagar are cities that are located in the Indian state of Gujarat. Gujarat is located along the coastlines of Indian Ocean in western India.
2  Sachin is a town which is located in city of Surat in Gujarat.
3  *Tazias* are decorative miniatures of the tomb of Imam Husain that are carried by the Muslims on their shoulders during the festival of Muharram to be immersed in the seas or other nearby water bodies.
4  A term used to refer to the low caste Hindus in India.

5  In Hinduism, Sithamman is regarded as the spiritual incarnation of Sitha, the wife of Lord Rama.

6  Goddess Durga is regarded as the symbol of feminine power and energy.

7  Lord Shiva is regarded as the god of destruction of evils.

8  Here, it is crucial to highlight that, traditionally, the usage of lemons is a common practice among the Hindus like hanging lemons outside homes to ward off evils, offering them to gods and goddesses during worships, etc. But, lemons are not commonly used as garlands during the Hindu rituals and this particular practice has been adapted by the indentured Hindus in South Africa (especially in Durban) from the Zulus.

9  A traditional Indian soup which evolved in southern India and is prepared with lentils, drumsticks, and various vegetables.

10  Gengaiamman is a water goddess who is associated to the river Ganga.

11  In 1994, the all-male temple committee in Pietermaritzburg banned the participation of women in fire-walking rituals. It led to a huge uproar among Hindu women across South Africa who continuously protested to uplift this ban. After a series of protests and conflicts, the ban was uplifted in 1999 (Diesel 2007, 202–208).

12  Located in the Bhavnagar district of Gujarat.

13  Abyssinia is the ancient name of Ethiopia.

14  Nubian Valley covers the present-day regions of Egypt and Sudan.

15  A spiritual event that marks the death anniversary of a Sufi saint.

16  Dargahs are referred to shrines or tombs that are built over the graves of revered spiritual figures.

17  Spiritual specialists.

18  *Dhamals* are a form of song and dance that are performed by the Siddis in Gujarat. Dhamals are of two types—*"Baithaaki Dhamal"* and "Dance *Dhamal."* The *"Baithaaki Dhamal"* is performed in the sitting position and the "Dance *Dhamal"* is performed in both sitting and standing positions. During the performance of *"Baithaaki Dhamal"* the focus lies more on the lyrics and less on the musical instruments and during the performance of "Dance *Dhamal"* the focus lies more on the sounds of the various musical instruments and less on the lyrics. During "Dance *Dhamal"* the musical instruments are often played in a frenzied manner. The frenzied music is accompanied by frenzied dance movements.

19  Spiritual hymns in Islam.

20  Hindu goddess of wealth.

21  "Teen Darwaza" or three gates were one of the many entrances to the kingdom of Ahmad Shah Badshah in Ahmedabad.

22  A goddess located in the seaside of Kuda and is associated with the oceanic spiritual myths of Gujarat.

# References

Baderoon, G. 2014. *Regarding Muslims: From Slavery to Post-apartheid*. Johannesburg: Wits University Press.

Badshah, O. 2022. 'Creolized Spiritual Practices of the Indians in South Africa'. Personal Conversation. Cape Town.

Basu, H. 2019. 'Narratives of Transcendental Decision-Making: Seeking Health and Healing at Sufi Shrines in Gujarat'. In *Knowledge and the Indian Ocean: Intangible Networks of Western India and Beyond*, edited by Sarah Keller, 190–204. New York: Palgrave.

Breteque, P.A. de la. 2021. 'Creolization as Cultural and Poetical Rebirth in "Arrival of the Snake-Woman" by Oliver Senior'. *Commonwealth Essays and Studies* 44, no. 1: 1–17.

de Silva, S. 2016. 'Lost Narratives and Hybrid Identities in the Indian Ocean: Afro-Asians'. *Indi@logs* 4: 11–26.

Devroop, C. 2022. 'Creolized Spiritual Practices of the Indians in South Africa'. Personal Conversation. Pretoria.

Diesel, A. 2007. *Shakti: Stories of Indian Women in South Africa.* Johannesburg: Wits University Press.

Freund, B. 1995. *Insiders and Outsiders: The Indian Working Class of Durban 1910–1990.* Natal: University of Natal Press.

Glissant, E. 1997. *Poetics of Relation. Translated by Betsy Wing.* Ann Arbor: University of Michigan Press.

Govender, R. 2022. 'Creolized Spiritual Practices of the Indians in South Africa'. Personal Conversation. Durban.

Henning, C.G. 1993. *The Indentured Indian in Natal (1860–1917).* New Delhi: Promilla & Co. Publishers.

Hofmeyr, I. 2020. 'The Sodden Archive: Africa, the Atlantic and the Indian Ocean'. In *Indian Ocean Histories: The Many Worlds of Michael Naylor Pearson*, edited by Rila Mukherjee and Radhika Seshan, 32–47. London & New York: Routledge.

Jeychandran, N. 2019. 'Navigating African Sacred Geography: Shrines for African Sufi Saints and Spirits in India'. *Journal of Africana Religions* 7, no. 1: 17–36.

Kumar, P.P. 2012. 'Hinduism in South Africa'. In *The Wiley-Blackwell Companion to African Religions*, edited by Elias Kifon Bongmba and Jacob K. Olupona, 389–398. Chicester: Blackwell Publishing Limited.

Lal, V. and Vahed, G. 2013. 'Hinduism in South Africa: Caste, Ethnicity, and Invented Traditions, 1860-Present'. *Journal of Sociology and Social Anthropology* 4, no. 1–2: 1–15.

Meer, F. 1969. *Portrait of Indian South Africans.* Durban: Avon House.

Mehta, M. 2019. 'Gujarat Sufis, "Sants" and the Indian Ocean World in Medieval Times'. In *Knowledge and the Indian Ocean: Intangible Networks of Western India and Beyond*, edited by Sarah Keller, 163–172. New York: Palgrave.

Ndlovu-Gatsheni, S.J. 2020. 'The Dynamics of Epistemological Decolonisation in the 21st Century: Towards Epistemic Freedom'. *Strategic Review for Southern Africa* 40, no. 1: 16–45.

Shroff, B. 2019. 'Voices of the Siddis: Indians of African Descent'. In *Knowledge and the Indian Ocean: Intangible Networks of Western India and Beyond*, edited by Sarah Keller, 205–224. New York: Palgrave.

Siddi, Farooq Murima. 2022a. 'About Siddi Folklores and Zikrs'. Personal Conversation. Ahmedabad.

Siddi, Hameeda Makwa. 2022b. 'About Spirit-Possession and Fire-Walking'. Personal Conversation. Ahmedabad.

Siddi, Qayyum Murima. 2022c. 'About Siddi Folklores and Zikrs'. Personal Conversation. Jamnagar.

Uimonen, P and Masimbi, H. 2021. 'Spiritual Relationality in Swahili Ocean Worlds'. *Swedish Journal of Anthropology* 4, no. 2: 35–50.

Wilson, R.S. 2022. 'Introduction: Worlding Asia Pacific into Oceania – Worlding Concepts, Tactics, and Transfigurations against the Anthropocene'. In *Geo-Spatiality in Asian and Oceanic Literature and Culture: Worlding Asia in the Anthropocene*, edited by S.S. Chou et al., 1–31. Ithaca: Cornell University Press.

# Chapter 4

# MUSICAL AND DANCE MEMORIES

## Introduction: Creole Musicscapes and the Indian Ocean

When the indentured Indians boarded the ships to Natal and the African slaves boarded the ships to Gujarat, along with many items, they carried musical instruments like *Dhamama*, *Musindo*,[1] *Dhol*,[2] *Misr Kanga*, *Malunga*,[3] Harmonium,[4] and several others (Figure 9). Philip Howard Colomb, in his book *Slave-catching in the Indian Ocean* (1873), observes that when the African slaves traveled by ships to India, they would engage in "frantic performances" (p. 280) in the forms of dancing, singing, and playing their musical instruments loudly. On a similar

**Figure 9:** Musical instrument room in the Dargah of Bava Gor in Jamnagar. The instruments are Mugarman, Musindo, Conch Shells and Malunga.

note, Chats Devroop, while talking about the creolized musical cultures of the South African Indians, shared that during long journeys to Natal, one of the ways in which the Indians entertained themselves on the ships was by singing, dancing, and playing musical instruments (2022). The musical and dance engagements of the Siddis and the South African Indians on the ships have intergenerationally passed on, got intermingled with local musical and dance cultures, and gave birth to creole musical and dance practices. On the one side, the creole musical and dance practices have allowed the Siddis in Gujarat and the South African Indians in South Africa to carve out a unique noncompartmentalized cultural space of their own, which cannot be imprisoned within the parameters of the mainstream[5] cultural enclaves, and on the other side, the creolized musical and dance practices function as the "reterritorialization of the multiplicities of sensation" (Roy 2018, p. 173) for these communities. From the ships across the Indian Ocean to the present-day cultural spaces, the reterritorialization of the multiplicities of emotions for these communities have sociohistorically taken place through maintaining the ancestral musical traditions as well as acknowledging the local musical and dance traditions.

The evolution of any form of creolized musical and dance practices is not a disconnection from the roots of the original musical and dance traditions but an opening up of cultural possibilities of porosities, fluidities, and endless continuities because "every enactment of tradition opens tradition to transformation" (Waterman 1990, p. 8). In the process of the transformation, the "present becomes past and the future present" (Martin 2013, p. 23), and as a result, the usual practice of interpreting mainstream musical and dance traditions as superior to the various ancestral musical and dance traditions of different indigenous communities gets questioned. The interrogations allow communities like the South African Indians, Siddis, and others to weave "in-between" musical and dance spaces of their own that are "invitational" and "resistant" at the same time. To elaborate further, the creolized musical spaces of the Siddis and the South African Indians make every effort to disintegrate the various social, cultural, and territorial hierarchies of musical and dance practices that exist around them by inviting other communities and their cultures into their respective cultural spaces. However, the invitation is made without comprising with the ancestral cultural and musical roots from where their creolized musical practices have evolved. Any form of assimilationist tendencies from within these communities and outside are firmly resisted. During my field research, the simultaneous performance of invitation and resistance was categorically visible when across Ahmedabad, Jamnagar, Bhavnagar, Durban, Pretoria, Cape Town, and Johannesburg, the Siddi and South African Indian community members wholeheartedly invited me to participate in their community dances and musical performances, but made sure that I follow the patterns of their performances as accurately as possible, without distorting them.

The Indian Ocean and its littorals, besides leading to the evolution of multiple sacredscapes in South Africa and Gujarat, as reflected in Chapter 3, also led to the evolution of several creolized musicscapes in the forms of *Dhamal* dance, *Goma*[6] dance, chutney music, band music, orchestra music, Indo-Afro-Jazz, and others. In Chapter 6, the practice of *Dhamal* in the form of zikrs have been discussed, and in this chapter, *Dhamal* as a dance form has been discussed. Before discussing the diverse creolized musical and dance practices of the Siddis and the South African Indians, let us very briefly look into the general state of creolized musical practices in Gujarat and South Africa prior to the arrival of these communities.

According to the various historical records, the creolization of musical practices in South Africa dates back to 1497, when Vasco da Gama reached the shores of what is known as Mossel Bay[7] today. Vasco da Gama and his fellow travelers were welcomed and entertained "by a group of Khoikhoi[8] musicians using the hocket technique on their flutes, which had been extremely popular among European composers [...] at the end of Middle Ages" (Martin 2013, p. 53). Later on, when *Vereenigde Nederlandsche Geoctroyeerde Oostindische Compagnie* (VOC)[9] arrived and settled in the Cape of Good Hope, "the first Commander of the Cape, Jan Van Riebeeck, is said to have regaled a Hottentot[10] Chief with a concert of the harpsichord" (Kirby 1937, p. 25). Such incidents regularized the interaction between European music and local indigenous music and laid the foundation of creolized musical cultures in South Africa. With the establishment of British colonization and the arrival of the Indian plantation workers in the Cape, the creolized musical space diversified further. The arrival of the Indian plantation workers in the Cape through the Indian Ocean and the Indian plantation workers in the Caribbean Islands through the Atlantic Ocean was a simultaneous process. In fact, many Indian plantation workers from the Cape were transferred to the Caribbean islands at different points of time. This simultaneous presence of Indian plantation workers in the Cape and the Caribbean islands widely transformed the existing creolized musicscape in South Africa through imbibing the culture of "chutney music" from the Indian plantation workers in the Caribbean. With the introduction of Indian chutney music in South Africa, the creolization of musical practices was not restricted to European musical patterns and the local indigenous African musical patterns anymore.

Besides chutney musicians, many Indians emerged successful as jazz musicians, orchestra musicians, and ballroom dancers during the 1950s in South Africa. For instance, Sony Pillai and Gambi George were well-known

Indian jazz musicians, and Runga Naidoo was a reputed ballroom dancer in Durban (Naidoo 2008, pp. 34–35). They dismantled the usual belief that ballroom dancing is exclusively meant for the Europeans and Jazz is exclusively meant for the blacks and the colored. The orchestra music was performed by the music bands of indentured laborers and railway workers like the Papiah Brothers, The Railway Youth Orchestral Club, The Golden Lily Orchestra, and others, who blended "Hindustani and Carnatic folk and classical traditions with American and European 'Big Band'[11] traditions" (Veeran 1996, p. 21). Their musical pieces were underlined with both "*raga*[12] and a sense of western harmony" (Veeran, p. 21). The next subsection elaborately reflects on the culture of chutney music and other forms of creolized musical and dance practices of the South African Indians today.

In the case of Gujarat in India, the evolution of creolized musical and dance practices can be traced back to the 13th century with the arrival of Alauddin Khilji from Afghanistan and the foundation of the Delhi Sultanate. The establishment of the Delhi Sultanate in Gujarat, besides various other cultural aspects, creolized the musical cultures of Gujarat through interweaving Hindu classical music and dance traditions with the Islamic classical music and dance traditions (Oppenheim 2019). With the establishment of the Muzaffarid dynasty in Gujarat in 14th century, the creolized musical and dance cultures in Gujarat underwent further diversification because the dynasty opened gateways for the arrival of Africans from eastern and northeastern parts of Africa as slaves, musicians, Sufi singers, gatekeepers, and palace guards (Perez 2020). A lot of Africans brought traditional musical instruments along with them, and as a result, their musical and dance patterns got intermingled with the existing Sufi musical and dance traditions of Gujarat that evolved through the spiritual leaders and Sufi singers who came to Gujarat from Persia (currently known as Iran), Baghdad (currently located in Iraq), and Assyria (currently known as Syria) mostly between 13th and 15th centuries. Today, within the Siddi community in Gujarat, *Garba*, African folk dances, *Goma* dance, *Dhaamal* dance, Sufi music, and *Dhaamal* music are performed in collaboration with each other. The creolized musical and dance practices of the Siddis in Gujarat have been discussed in the third subsection.

### From Distortion toward Creolization: Creole Musical Experiences of the South African Indians

During a personal conversation, Chats Devroop revealed that the creolized traditions of chutney music[13] developed through the half-baked imitation and distortion of Indian music by recording Hindi songs from the All

Indian Radio station of South Africa and/or listening to it repeatedly in the movie halls (2022). The songs in the chutney music are composed of "local Hindi Bhojpuri, pidgin English, and current slang" and they attack "the establishment and authority generally" (Jackson 1991, p. 182). During the performance of chutney songs, a wide array of classical Indian, traditional African and European musical instruments is used like harmonium, *dhol*, tanpura,[14] *tabla*,[15] cymbals, tambourine, drum, *musindo*, djembe, trumpet, and many others. Historically, for the indentured Indian community in South Africa, the chutney songs have functioned as an agency of voicing their pains and concerns against the dehumanizing sociopolitical policies of the European colonizers. The songs enabled them to acquire at least a "small degree of visibility" and most importantly made them realize the importance of their own voice and "who they are" (Rodgers et al. 2016, p. 88) in a foreign land.

Chats father ran a music band in Durban that played during the Hindu marriages in South Africa. As Chats shared, his father learned playing different musical instruments on his own without any official training. Chats also joined his father's band at the age of 12 and started learning different forms of musical instruments in the same way as his father did, before getting professionally trained in saxophone much later in his life. So, chutney music emerged through a technically untrained and rhythmically unstructured self-learning process.

Prior to the beginning of the Apartheid in 1948, when Indian musicians from India came to perform in South Africa, they were often requested by the South African Indians, to leave the instruments behind. In this way, the Indians got access to diverse forms of Indian classical musical instruments in South Africa, which was otherwise impossible. This is how; Chats father founded his music band. Another interesting aspect of chutney music in South Africa is the complex gender dynamics. During the late 19th century, the culture of chutney music evolved with the performance of folk songs that narrated stories from Hindu epics like Mahabharata, Ramayana, and others. The performances took place in Hindi, Bhojpuri, and Natal-Bhojpuri.[16] The performances were only conducted by men because during that time the participation of Indian women on the stage were regarded as socioculturally abhorrent. So, the roles of women were played by the men, who cross-dressed as women and transgenders. The chutney music was accompanied by dances and the male cross-dressers, who comically imitated the women and the transgenders to make the audience laugh. This process of imitation ridiculed the women and the transgenders on the one side, and opened gateways for the gay South African Indians to participate in the creative sociocultural spaces of South Africa on the other. Though gay-bashing continues to take place in South Africa, but it has been widely challenged by the participation of gay South African Indians in chutney songs. Today, the chutney musicians in South Africa mostly perform self-composed Hindi songs and Bollywood songs by mixing with pop, jazz, Indian folk, and local South African musical practices. For instance, AAFRIND is a South Africa-based chutney music band that performs fusions of Indian, African, and European music. The band performs creole mashups by blending popular Bollywood songs with traditional African and classical European songs and musical patterns.

Unlike chutney music, due to various economic and cultural challenges,[17] the musical practices of jazz and orchestra did not survive for long among the indentured Indian community. At present, jazz is commonly performed by the native blacks in jazz festivals and other music festivals in South Africa. With only a few South African Indian musicians and musicians from other communities in South Africa, orchestras are also commonly performed in the music festivals. Nisaar Pangarker, a resident of Cape Town and Founder and Director of Inner Circle Entertainment, during a personal conversation, shared how his organization in South Africa has been curating shows on Indian classical music and fusion orchestras with local South African and international musicians since 2004 (Pangarker 2022). In the fusion orchestras, different musical patterns like Indian classical, African folk, and jazz are interwoven and creolized. For instance, a creole orchestra performance called "Raga Afrika" was curated at the North Sea Jazz Festival in Cape Town in 2004, which consisted of a fusion performance of Indian classical and Afro-Jazz. During the performance, the musical instruments that were played are sitar,[18] violin, electric guitar, *tabla*, drums, and synthesizer (Inner Circle Entertainment 2020).[19] The performance unpacked the different aspects of the classical musical culture of India and the jazz musical culture of South Africa simultaneously.

Besides creole songs and orchestras, creole dance practices have widely shaped the cultural identities of the South African Indians in South Africa, especially for the South African Indian women. Suria Govender, a fusion dancer from Durban and the founder of the SuriaLanga[20] Dance Company, creolizes Bharatanatyam[21] with traditional Zulu dance forms. During a personal conversation, Suria argued that creole dance forms question the notion of "cultural ownership" (2022) of different communities because through creolization a person cannot be chauvinistic about a particular cultural form and need to embrace multiple forms of cultural practices in a borderless manner. In her dance company she has both Indian and Zulu students, and they learn Bharatanatyam and traditional Zulu dances simultaneously. She also shared that when Nelson Mandela was coronated as the first black president of postapartheid South Africa, she and her dance troupe was invited to perform. Her troupe consisted of both Indian and Zulu dancers, who performed a fusion of Bharatanatyam and traditional Zulu dance with the song "Asimbonanga."[22] Creolizing an Indian classical dance form with an indigenous African dance form has enabled Suria Govender and his company members to carve out a multi-rooted, transoceanic, and transcontinental cultural space for their respective communities on the one side, and re-weave the broken threads of cultural collaborations and cohabitations that existed prior to the imposition of the group areas acts during the apartheid era on the other.

Apart from the SuriaLanga Dance Company, the Siwela Sonke Dance Theatre (SSDT) in Durban has been developing creolized dance patterns since 1994 by interweaving "Contemporary African Dance, Traditional African Dance, Contemporary Modern Dance, Traditional Indian Dance, and Classical Ballet" (Singh 2019, p. 124). The SSDT not only performs on the stages, but also in "public spaces where there is free access, with a strong focus on community development" (Singh, p. 124) and a culturally and racially diverse coexistence.

Vasugi Dewar Singh and Siddharthiya Pillai from Durban have also been contributing toward the creolized dance culture of South Africa. Vasugi Dewar Singh, a South African Indian classical dancer from Durban was among the first group of Indian dancers from South Africa, who went to India to seek training in Bharatanatyam in the 1970s. After receiving training for a couple of years, she returned back to South Africa and started training a lot of Indians and black Africans in the traditional Bharatanatyam dance form.

Siddharthiya Pillai, who is also from Durban, got trained in Kathak[23] and Bharatanatyam in South Africa. Though, like Vasugi, she is more inclined toward traditional Bharatanatyam dance forms, she has curated several contemporary performance styles like performing "Bharatanatyam with Zulu poetry," "Bharatanatyam with miscellaneous traditional African dance forms," and others (Pillai 2022). She believes that the performance of creolized contemporary dance forms has enabled the South African Indian communities to dismantle the caste, cultural, and racial hierarchies in South Africa to a vast extent, because such dance forms assist in building invitational transcultural spaces and collaborative cultural relationships, without obliterating and violating the cultural differences.

On the whole, the creolized musical and dance practices of the South African Indians have sociohistorically empowered them to "negotiate, order and control the boundaries and expressions of Indian diasporic identities" and contribute to the "new contestations and dilemmas" that have evolved with respect to the sociocultural transformations in postapartheid South Africa (Dickinson 2014, p. 32). The discussions on creolized musical and dance practices continue to take place in the following subsection in the context of the Siddis in Gujarat.

## Creole Musical Practices of the Siddis in Gujarat

"Koi bhi Siddi hoga, paele usko rhythm aur gana ata hain" (Everybody in the Siddi community is born with a sense of rhythm and music).

(Rafiq Murima Siddi 2022)

In the article "Recollecting Africa" (2000), Edward Alpers observes that "wherever Africans were moved in the diaspora of the eastern hemisphere, they carried their music and dance with them," which in the long run have "become integrated-sometimes centrally-into the culture of different host societies" (p. 90). The musical practices of the Siddis in Gujarat in the forms of songs and dances have undergone creolization in the same way. Apart from interweaving Sufi spiritual practices with traditional African (mostly east African and northeast African) spiritual traditions, the Siddis have also inherited the zikr singing tradition of the Sufis. The rhythms of their songs are developed according to the zikr signing tradition, and traditional east African and northeast African percussion instruments like *Goma*[24] and *Mugarman*[25] are used as accompaniments. The *Goma* drum is similar to the *Ngoma* drum,[26] (Figure 10) which is played across different parts of Africa. *Ngoma* is a small cylindrical drum and is played in the same way as *Goma*. The zikr singing tradition of the Siddis have been elaborately discussed in Chapter 3.

The creolized musical practices of the African Indians in Gujarat also function as an effective space for feminine empowerment. During the *urs* of Bava Gor, the women from the African Indian community in Gujarat dance and sing songs for Mai Misra (sister of Bava Gor) (Figure 11). This repertoire of worship is known as *Mai na garba*[27] or *garba* for Mai Misra. Originally, *garba* is performed to worship Goddess Amba Mata[28] in Gujarat and the "Siddi women have adapted *garba* to honour Mai Mishra" (Shroff 2019, p. 217). During the *Mai na garba*, the Siddi women sing zikrs and qawwalis, and play the bead rattles. The bead rattles are also played by many African indigenous communities in eastern and other parts of Africa to keep up with the rhythm of the songs. The bead rattles are also used by the Siddi fakirs to bless the passersby.

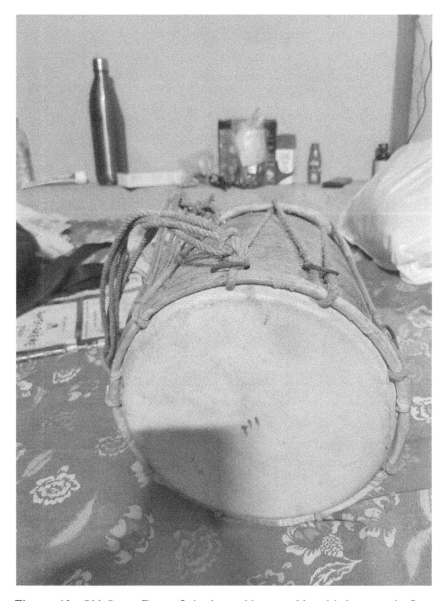

**Figure 10:** Old Goma Drum. It is almost 90 years old and belongs to the Late Rumana Makwa Siddi in Patthar Kuwa, Ahmedabad.

During the various spiritual and cultural rituals, along with the *Goma* and *Mugarman* drums, the African Indians perform the *Goma* and *Dhamal* dance. The hand and the body movements of the African Indian *Dhamal* and *Goma* dancers in Gujarat are very similar to the *Ngoma* dancers in Africa. The *Ngoma*

**Figure 11:** Mugurmans. Inside the shrine of Bava Gor in Ahmedabad.

dancers thump their feet and swing their arms sideways with the rhythm of *Ngoma* drums. The *Dhamal* and *Goma* dancers in Gujarat also swing their arms sideways, but thumping of feet depends on the contexts of their dance. During religious occasions the *Dhamal* dance is performed and feet-thumping does not take place. It is so, because, as discussed in Chapter 3, the Siddis follow many spiritual aspects of the Sufi tradition to worship Bava Gor and Mai Misra. The word *Dhamal* has been inherited from the Sufi word *Damal*, which refers to "different types of Sufi music and dancing that commonly involves experiences of ecstasy and spirit possession" (Shroff 2019, p. 212). The hand and body movements of the *Dhamal* dancers convey spiritual ecstasy and transition. For instance, while documenting a performance of dance *Dhamal* on September 10, 2022, I observed that the Siddi dancers were dancing to the zikrs of Bava Gor and the dance movements imitated the body languages of the wild animals, the existential patterns of the trees in the forests, and the movement of the rivers and the oceans. The culture of imitating the body languages, existential patterns, and the movements of the different living beings in the natural environment during the *Dhamal* dances is associated with the Afro-Indian creole spiritual folklores that talk about how Bava Gor along with his sister Mai Misra and five other siblings came to Gujarat from Ethiopia, through the Nubian Valley and the Indian Ocean, and traveled across forests and rivers in Gujarat to spiritually enrich the Siddis and other people.

In case the *Goma*[29] dance is performed, along with imitating the movements of different living beings in the natural environment, feet-thumping is common. Such a way of performing *Goma* dance is commonly found among the Siddis, who stay around the Gir Forest National Park of Gujarat. In the course of the *Goma* performances, the Siddis centrally imitate the body movements and the hunting patterns of the lions, the zebras, the ostriches, and other animals and birds that are found in the Gir Forest National Park (United Nations 2017; Siddi 2022). Such performances are identical to the *Ngoma* dancers in Africa, who, through their dances imitate, the calls, and the body movements of the animals and birds (New World Encyclopedia contributors 2021). In addition to *Goma* drums, *Mugarman* drums, *Goma* dances, *Dhamal* dances, bead rattles, and the playing of *Malunga* (a single-string instrument of African origin) is also prevalent in the Creole musical culture of the Siddis in Gujarat. *Malunga* is mostly played by the Siddi *fakirs* in the villages of Gujarat. While playing the *Malunga*, the Siddis sing *zikrs* of Bava Gor and Mai Misra, walk around the villages, and seek donations. The donations are not only made by the Muslims, but by people from other religious communities as well. This is how, the transoceanic creole musical practices of the Siddis in Gujarat celebrate communal harmony.

Ernie Nathi Koela, a researcher from South Africa, in his research on centrally braced bow musical instruments notes the transoceanic and the transcontinental connection of *Malunga* with Africa by identifying that the appearance and the playing pattern of a *Malunga* is similar to a *Chitende* in Mozambique and a *uMakhweyana* in KwaZulu-Natal in South Africa (2019,

p. 14). Ernie also observes that *Malunga, Chitende,* and *uMakhweyana* are made in the same way. These instances of the creolized musical and dance practices of the Siddis in Gujarat show that the performance styles of the Siddis are embedded in the "African-derived cosmologies" and the "Sufi discourse" at the same time (Basu 2008, p. 292).

The creolized musical and dance practices of the Siddis and the South African Indians have generated multiple sites of "transnational and translocal belongings" across the Indian Ocean (Dickinson 2014, p. 33). The transnational and translocal cultural sites have reproduced the "ancestral cultural traditions" and recreated a "homeplace in new settings" for these communities (Dickinson, p. 33). The present relationship between these communities and their countries of origin across the Indian Ocean is "tense, ambivalent, yet cultivated relationship, as both sides appreciate the material and cognitive value of the link but have been transformed by the experience of separation" (Akyeampong 2000, p. 188).

But, today, the musical and dance practices of these communities have been affected by assimilations, distortions, and hierarchies. The following subsection argues how the musical and dance practices of these communities are assimilated and how the assimilations are resisted by the community members.

## Creole Music and Dance as Countercultures: Preserving Traditions and Resisting Assimilations

Having talked about the creolized dimension of the chutney musical culture of the South African Indians in South Africa, it is also crucial to unpack the often-invisible forms of hierarchies that exist between the performers in terms of the selection of languages, stories, and the performance patterns of the chutneys. At the beginning of the evolution of chutney music, a majority of the chutney songs were composed and sung by the indentured laborers who came from the states of Bihar and Uttar Pradesh in North India. The indentured laborers, who came from the southern parts of India, hardly acknowledged and participated in this form of music because many regarded the chutney music as a distortion of the traditional Indian culture. The southern Indian indentured laborers concentrated in maintaining their traditional Indian cultures as firmly as possible. Therefore, spiritually and culturally, they tried to maintain a strong community bonding among themselves. So, the chutney musical performances in South Africa were in Hindi, Bhojpuri, and Natal-Bhojpuri. Today, the chutney musicians of South Africa mostly perform Bollywood songs and many believe that the earlier songs, which centered on religious narratives, are backdated now. They perform during marriages and cultural festivals. The contemporary performances are mostly assisted by dances that imitate the Bollywood-styled and party-styled popular dance forms of India. But, there a few musical groups who continue to preserve the old traditional ways of performing spiritual chutney songs by blending Indian folk style and *kirtaniya* style[30] with the local South African ones. Such groups mostly perform during specific Hindu religious and cultural festivals in South Africa. Despite these hierarchies, it is needless to say, that consistent efforts are being made to preserve and practice this traditional creolized musical practice by the South African Indians. Apart from the physical performances, the social media platforms like YouTube, Facebook, Instagram, and others play a crucial role in promoting chutney music of South Africa across the globe. For instance, YouTube channels like "Chutney Music," Facebook groups like "SA Indian Chutney," and Instagram communities like "chutney.music" and "chutney_music_worldwide" have been playing an instrumental role toward promoting the chutney musical culture of South Africa worldwide. Several musical groups from South Africa also perform at chutney music festivals across the world.

Similar to chutney music, the creolized musical practices with respect to *Dhamal* dance and *Goma* dance have undergone similar transformations with time. Today, in order to gain the attention of the tourists, music producers, and event managers, many Siddi musicians and dancers have disowned the original traditional ways of performing the *Dhamal* and *Goma* dances, and perform them in a stereotypically loud and frenzied manner that fits into the universally preconceived problematic notion that all forms of African music and dances are loud and frenzied in nature. Such forms of stereotypical performances are resisted by many Siddi community members who believe that the distortions of their original musical and dance patterns will lead to cultural assimilations and erasures. The Siddi organizations like Siddi Goma Al-Mubrik Charitable Trust in Bhavnagar, Samast Sidi Jamat in Jamnagar, and Siddi Education Mandal and Siddi Mai Misra Pragati Mahila Mandal in Ahmedabad have been making consistent efforts to sensitize the Siddis about their music, dance, spiritual worship, and ancestral knowledge systems, and epistemologically and ontologically equip them to resist the seductions of cultural assimilations and distortions.

Despite these challenges, it is needless to say that the creolized musical practices of the South African Indians and the Siddis have generated multiple "countercultures of modernity" (Gilroy 1993, p. 82), which cannot be imprisoned within the predecided, hierarchical, and culturally excluded mainstream musical and dance traditions of India and South Africa. Unlike many mainstream musical and dance traditions, the creolized musical and dance practices of these communities do not make any effort to erase the cultural differences in India and South Africa, but "underwrite a complex process of making connections" (Nuttal and Michael 2000, p. 10). The discussions on creolization, collaborations, and resistance of the South African Indians and the Siddis continue to take place in Chapter 5 through their creolized culinary practices.

## Endnotes

1  It is a percussion instrument and it looks similar to the traditional Indian percussion instrument "Dhol."
2  A double-headed Indian drum.
3  A single-string musical instrument made of wood and goat skin.
4  A free-reed keyboard traditional Indian instrument.
5  In this chapter, I have used to the word "mainstream" to refer to the musical traditions in India and South Africa that are regarded as "important" and "valuable" on the basis of their commercial viability and not on the basis of historical, traditional, and cultural values.
6  *Goma* is a dance form that are commonly performed by the Siddis in Gujarat and has been inherited from their eastern African and northeastern African ancestors.
7  A town located in South Africa's Western Cape province.
8  An indigenous group of people from South Africa and Namibia.
9  *Vereenigde Nederlandsche Geoctroyeerde Oostindische Compagnie* (VOC) is the Dutch name for the Dutch East India Company.
10  The term "Hottentot" is a racially abusive term that was used by the Dutch to refer to the Khoikhoi and San people of South Africa and Namibia. In the Dutch language, "Hottentot" means "to stammer/stutter." The Khoisan language (the native language of the Khoikhoi and the San people) is full of click sounds. As the Dutch did not understand the click sounds in the Khoisan language, they misinterpreted the click sounds as speech defects of the Khoikhoi and San people. As a result, they were referred to as "Hottentots."
11  Big Band is a form of musical ensemble of jazz music that started during the early 1910s in the United States and usually consisted of ten and more musicians. The musicians were divided across four sections: saxophones, trombones, trumpets, and a rhythm section.
12  In Indian classical music, while singing, playing musical instruments, and dancing, different notes in the rhythms signify different emotional experiences. Such notes are referred to as *ragas*.
13  The term chutney music is used to refer to a form of Indian creolized music in South Africa, which like a chutney, is a mixture of different genres of music like pop, jazz, blues, and Indian folk.
14  A long-necked plucked string instrument which has originated in India.
15  An Indian classical percussion instrument.
16  Natal-Bhojpuri is a Creole language that emerged among the Indian indentured laborers in Natal, who arrived from the northern Indian state of Bihar, through their interaction with the local Zulu and Bantu communities in the sugarcane plantations and mines. Natal Bhojpuri is a mixture of the Bhojpuri language (a native language of

Bihar) and the local Zulu and Bantu languages. With the evolution of chutney music in South Africa, many chutney songs were sung in this language. Today, the language is hardly spoken anymore.

17 Most of the instruments that are played in jazz and orchestra are western instruments and therefore they are expensive. The process of getting trained in jazz and orchestra is expensive as well. As a result, it has been difficult for many Indians to afford the whole process of purchasing instruments and getting trained. Moreover, unlike chutney music, a lot of South African Indians have felt socioculturally distant from jazz and orchestra, as the lyrics and the musical patterns do not connect much to their social, cultural, and historical roots.

18 Like tanpura, sitar is also a classical Indian plucked string instrument.

19 A glimpse of the performance can be accessed through the following link: https://www.facebook.com/innercircleentertainment/videos/3051297764986219/ ?extid=CL-UNK-UNK-UNK-AN_GK0T-GK1C&ref=sharing.

20 The name "SuriaLanga" is also creole in nature. The words "Suria" and "Langa" means "sun" and they belong to two different languages. In the Hindi language the sun is called "Suria" and in the Zulu language the sun is called "Langa."

21 An Indian classical dance form that originated in the southern Indian state of Tamil Nadu.

22 "Asimbonanga" is an anti-apartheid song in the Zulu language and was dedicated to Nelson Mandela. The song was released when Nelson Mandela, along with many other anti-apartheid activists, were imprisoned in the Robben Island.

23 A type of Indian classical dance that evolved in the northern Indian state of Uttar Pradesh.

24 *Goma* is a small cylindrical one-sided drum and is played by hanging from the shoulders with both hands. *Goma* is the name of an Afro-Indian dance form as well. To further understand the way in which a *Goma* drum is played, go to the following link: https://www.youtube.com/shorts/1nyGyf_0dx4.

25 A large cylindrical one-sided hand drum. The drum is placed in the standing position on the floor and is played with both hands. To further understand the way in which a *Mugarman* is played, go to the following link: https://www.youtube.com/ watch?v=404cN3HjrVg.

26 *Ngoma* is the name of an African dance form as well.

27 *Garba* is a traditional folk singing and dancing form of Gujarat, during which the dancers sing and dance in a circular manner with sticks in hands. The sticks are played against each other by the performers and are synced with the body movements.

28 "Amba Mata" is the incarnation of Goddess *Durga*, who is the spiritual symbol of motherhood and feminine power.

29 The dancing patterns of both the *Goma* dance and the *Dhamal* dance are almost similar, with a few differences. The *Dhamal* dance is specifically performed during the religious rituals of Bava Gor and Mai Misra, while the *Goma* dance is not performed during the religious rituals and performed on other occasions by the Siddis. During the *Dhamal* dance, feet thumping does not take place, which is quite common in the *Goma* dance. The body movements of the Siddi dancers during the *Dhamal* dance imitate the movements of the animals, trees, rivers, and the oceans. While performing *Goma* dance, the body movements of the dancers centrally imitate the body movements and the hunting patterns of the different wild animals.

30  *Kirtaniya* is a traditional form of Indian music that evolved within the Hindu spiritual-musical order of North India and is performed during specific religious festivals, mostly in North India.

## References

Akyeampong, E. 2000. 'Africans in the Diaspora: The Diaspora and Africa'. *African Affairs* 99, no. 395: 183–215.

Alpers, E. 2020. 'Recollecting Africa: Diasporic Memory in the Indian Ocean World'. *African Studies Review* 43, no. 1: 83–99.

Basu, H. 2008. 'Drumming and Praying: Sidi at the Interface between Spirit Possession and Islam'. In *Struggling with History: Islam and Cosmopolitanism in the Western Indian Ocean*, edited by E. Simpson and K. Kresse, 291–322. Columbia: Columbia University Press.

Colomb, P.H. 1873. *Slave-Catching in the Indian Ocean: A Record of Naval Experiences.* London: Longmans, Green & Co.

Devroop, C. 2022. 'Creole Musical Practices of the South African Indians in South Africa'. Personal Conversation. Pretoria.

Dickinson, J. 2014. 'Making Space for India in Post-apartheid South Africa: Narrating Diasporic Subjectivities through Classical Song and Dance'. *Emotion, Space and Society* 13: 32–39.

Gilroy, P. 1993. *The Black Atlantic: Modernity and Double Consciousness.* Harvard: Harvard University Press.

Govender, S. 2022. 'Creole Dance Practices of the South African Indians in South Africa'. Personal Conversation. Durban.

Inner Circle Entertainment. 2020. 'Inner Circle Entertainment' [2004] 14 May. Available at: https://www.facebook.com/innercircleentertainment/videos/30512977 64986219/?extid=CL-UNK-UNK-UNK-AN_GK0T-GK1C&ref=sharing (Accessed 3 November 2022).

Jackson, M. 1991. 'Popular Indian South African Music: Division in Diversity'. *Popular Music* 10, no. 2: 175–188.

Kirby, P.R. 1937. 'Saint Cecilia Goes South (A Contribution to the History of Music in South Africa)'. *Proceedings of the Musical Association*, 64th Session: 25–38.

Koela, E.N. 2019. '"Seeds of the Braced Bow": (The Flower, the Seed and the Bee)'. PhD diss., University of Cape Town, 2019. https://open.uct.ac.za/bitstream/ handle/11427/31398/thesis_hum_2019_koela_ernie_nathi.pdf?sequence=-1&isAllowed=y.

Martin, D-C. 2013. *Sounding the Cape: Music, Identity and Politics in South Africa.* Somerset West: African Minds.

Naidoo, R. 2008. *The Indian in Drum Magazine in the 1950s.* Johannesburg: Bell-Roberts Publishing.

New World Encyclopedia contributors. 2021. 'Africa Dance'. *New World Encyclopedia.* 30 April. https://www.newworldencyclopedia.org/p/index.php?title=African_ dance&oldid=1052074.

Nuttal, S. and Michael, C-A. 2000. *Senses of Culture, South African Culture Studies.* Oxford: Oxford University Press.

Oppenheim, M. 2019. *Genealogy, Archive, Image: Interpreting Dynastic History in Western India.* Warsaw: De Gruyter.

Pangarker, N. 2022. 'Creole Musical Practices of the South African Indians in South Africa'. Personal Conversation. Cape Town.

Perez, R.M. 2020. 'Subalternity across the Indian Ocean: The Sidis of Gujarat'. *Asian Review of World Histories* 8, no. 1: 61–82.

Pillai, S. 2022. 'Creole Dance Practices of the South African Indians in South Africa'. Personal Conversation. Durban.

Rodgers, A.P.L. et al. 2016. 'Song Memory as a Territory of Resistance Among South American Indigenous Peoples: A Collective Documentation Project'. *The World of Music* 5, no. 1: 81–110.

Roy, A.G. 2018. 'Transnational Bollywood Assemblages in Singapore'. In *Routledge Handbook of the Indian Diaspora*, edited by R. S. Hegde and A. K. Sahoo, 170–182. London and New York: Routledge.

Shroff, B. 2019. 'Voices of the Sidis: Indians of African Descent'. In *Knowledge and the Indian Ocean: Intangible Networks of Western India and Beyond*, edited by S. Keller, 205–224. New York: Palgrave Macmillan.

Siddi, Ravi. 2022. 'Goma Dance of the African Indians in Gir'. Personal Conversation. Gujarat.

Singh, V.D. 2019. *Bharathanatyam: A Journey from India to South Africa*. Durban: Atlas Printers.

United Nations. 2017. 'The Siddis: India's Forgotten Africans'. YouTube *video*, 8:41, February 21, 2017. https://www.youtube.com/watch?v=Q4SNsgwXsys.

Veeran, N.D. 1996. 'The Orchestral Traditions Amongst Indian South Africans in Durban between 1935 and 1970'. Master's thesis, University of Natal, 1996. https://researchspace.ukzn.ac.za/bitstream/handle/10413/8938/Veeran_Naresh_Denny_1996.pdf?sequence=1&isAllowed=y.

Waterman, C.A. 1990. *Juju, A Social History and Ethnography of an African Popular Music*. Chicago: The University of Chicago Press.

# Chapter 5

# CULINARY MEMORIES

## Introduction: Transoceanic Roots and Routes

Apart from various types of musical instruments, as discussed in Chapter 4, the African Indians and the South African Indians traveled to India and South Africa, respectively, with seeds and saplings of different traditional plants that are local to their respective geographical areas of origin. For instance, when the Indians arrived in South Africa, they carried saplings and seeds of basil, neem, curry leaf, mango, tamarind, and many others, while the Africans in India arrived with the seeds and saplings of baobab tree, lady finger, coffee beans, tomatoes, and many others. The seeds and the saplings were not just mere objects for these communities but functioned as cultural memories through which they could remain associated with their ancestral roots, even though they were physically displaced.

Today, in the states of Gujarat and Madhya Pradesh in India, the use of *Khorasani Imli* in vegetables, chutneys, and pickles are quite common. In the late Middle Ages, the Persian word "Khorasan" was used to denote the present-day country of Iran, and *Khorasani Imli* refers to the seeds of the Baobab tree that were brought to India by the Africans from eastern, northern, and southern Africa (whitehorsepress 2018). The Baobab seeds are referred to as *Khorasani* because they were brought by the Africans who came through Iran with the Islamic invaders as slaves and are referred to as *Imli* because they taste sour like tamarinds (known as *Imli* in the Hindi language). On an identical note, a lot of the houses of the South African Indians in South Africa (especially the Hindus), consists of mango trees, curry leaf plants, tamarind plants, and basil leave plants. It is so because, a majority of the indentured Indians came to South Africa from the southern parts of India, where tamarind and curry leaves are habitually used in cooking. Besides consuming tamarind and curry leaves, mango leaves and basil leaves are widely used in performing various religious, cultural, and spiritual rituals by South African Indian Hindus.

Before discussing further about the culinary practices of the Siddis in Gujarat and the South African Indians in Durban, Pretoria, and

Johannesburg, it is crucial to mention that the culinary practices of the Siddis in the contemporary era are no different from the local Indian communities. So, the culinary creoles of the Siddis can be located not in terms of the "ingredients" that they use to cook their food, but in terms of the transoceanic, transcontinental, and archipelagic "contexts" in which they prepare and consume their foods. To elaborate further, the culinary creoles of the Siddis can be contextually located within their spiritual practices.

## Culinary Creoles of the Siddis

During the spiritual practices, on the one side, their eastern African spiritual ancestors like Bava Gor, Mai Misra, Baba Habash, and others are worshipped according to African traditions, and on the other side, the spiritual ancestors are offered traditional Indian foods like khichdi, fish curry, sweet rice porridge, and others. Such a practice of interweaving African worshipping traditions and Indian culinary traditions invites us to understand the culinary creoles of the Siddis as an epistemological phenomenon and not just as a mere ontological phenomenon (Kabir 2023, p. 7). With respect to the established biological and linguistic definitions, the Siddis may not qualify as a creole community, but their spiritual, musical, and culinary practices have led to the evolution of creolized existential spaces through multicultural and transoceanic interactions. The culinary creoles of the Siddis in Gujarat vary from one region to another. In this chapter, the culinary creoles of the Siddis have been discussed with respect to my interactions with the Siddi community in Ahmedabad, Jamnagar, and Bhavnagar.

During conversations on the interlinks between the culinary practices and the spiritual practices of the Siddis, Farida Al-Mubrik from Bhavnagar, and Hameeda Makwa Siddi from Ahmedabad shared how during the *Urs* of Mai Misra, on the one hand Mai Misra's khichdi is prepared and on the other hand *Baithaaki Dhamal* is performed by the Siddi women. As already discussed in Chapter 4, the *Dhamal* is performed in the Gujarati, Hindi, Urdu, and Gujarati-Swahili Creole languages, and different eastern African musical instruments are played like *Musindo, Misr Kanga*, and *Mugarman*. Usually, the *Dhamal* that is sung during the preparation of khichdi is "Ya hoya, kya hoya?"[1] (Farida Al-mubrik and Hameeda Makwa Siddi 2022), and the khichdi is prepared in the traditional Indian style with rice and lentils by the Siddi women. Though khichdi in itself is not a creolized culinary preparation, but the phenomenon of culinary creole with respect to the preparation of khichdi during the *Urs* of Mai Misra can be broadly identified in two ways.

First, as the khichdi is prepared and the *Baithaaki Dhamals* are performed simultaneously, the Indian culinary significance of the khichdi gets interwoven with the Afro-Indian spiritual and musical significance of the *Dhamals*, and the khichdi attains a creole identity. After the preparation is complete, the khichdi is offered to Mai Misra, and then it is eaten by the Siddi women who prepared the khichdi. After they finish eating, the remaining khichdi is distributed among the other community members. As the Siddi women (who prepared the khichdi) eat, the other Siddi women continue to perform *Dhamals* by singing various *zikrs* of Mai Misra. As a transoceanic creole community, this simultaneous culinary, spiritual, and musical performance allows the Siddis to honor their eastern African ancestors on the one side and recognize the local Indian cultural tastes on the other.

Second, the preparation of khichdi is not only a culinary practice, but a spiritual practice, where the process of cooking, offering, and consuming the khichdi enables the Siddis to generate a metaphysical connection with their eastern African spiritual leaders and ancestors through their palates. The ritual of Mai Misra's khichdi (also known as *khicari*), which is a culinary item and a Sufi ritual at the same time, has "rich similarities with eastern African traditions of spirit possession such as *ngoma ya masheitani* or *zar* in contemporary Zanzibar or Sudan respectively" (Graves 2008, p. 1). The culinary preparation and the ceremony of Khichdi serve as a "site for communion between the spirits of northeast African Sufi saints and African Indians," (Graves, p. 1) who preserve the legacy of their ancestors through these practices.

A similar pattern of culinary creole can be identified during the *Urs* of Bava Gor, when *Ghava* is prepared and consumed, and simultaneously Afro-Indian zikrs are sung. Besides discussing about the ritual of khichdi, Farida and Hameeda also mentioned the ritual of preparing, offering, and consuming *Ghava* to Bava Gor. *Ghava* is a sweet dish that is prepared with semolina, milk, and sugar by the Siddi men inside a closed kitchen room. Usually, the kitchen room is located within the shrine of Bava Gor, and along with preparing the *Ghava*, the Siddis repeatedly sing the following zikr:

Halwa Gomey
Malwa Gomey (Al-Mubrik and Siddi 2022)

Until the preparation of *Ghava* is over, the Siddi men sing this zikr. The zikr means that the preparation of *Ghava* (also known as halwa) will spiritually satisfy Bav Gor, and the Siddi community will be wholeheartedly blessed by him. The culinary ritual of *Ghava*, like Mai Misra's khichdi, needs to be situated within a wider sociohistorical framework of the transoceanic, transcultural, and Afro-Indian creolized spiritual practices of the Siddis, where the palates, musical rhythms, and the spiritual values intersect with each other through "mobility, migration and personal encounters" (Breteque 2021, p. 2). The culinary-spiritual-musical constellation of the Siddi existence in Gujarat also unfolds a "mutual recognition of distinct territories and overlapping boundaries" (Ghosh 2021, p. 71) with the South African Indians in South Africa, who are otherwise separated by "geographical and historical injunctions" (dos Anjos 2008, p. 173). The overlapping sociocultural aspects has been further discussed in the following section.

## Culinary Creoles of the South African Indians

Though historically, the culinary cultures of the South African Indian community in South Africa and the Siddi community in Gujarat have evolved across different spatiotemporal moments and socioeconomic contexts, but the cultural imbrications in terms of how the respective culinary practices of both communities interweave with their respective spiritual practices cannot be ignored. The creole food habits and culinary practices have enabled the South African Indians to develop fluid transoceanic roots that are anchored both in India and South Africa and socially, culturally, and mnemonically expand across the Indian Ocean. The creolized culinary habits can be analyzed from two broad perspectives—creolization as a solution to crises and creolization as an acknowledgment of multicultural and multiracial existence.

### *From Crises to Creolization*

Since the period of indentureship, the South African Indian kitchen spaces "has been a site of harrowing intimacy, power, knowledge and invisible ideological contest" (Baderoon 2014, p. 50) in the forms of caste, class, and racial biases. The creolized culinary practices of the South African Indians are more visible among the Indians who trace their ancestry from the indentured laborers and less visible among the high-caste Hindu passenger Indians. It is also important to note that during the Apartheid era, the population of the indentured Indian laborers and the passenger Indians in South Africa were mostly composed of Hindus, with a few Muslims and Christians. As a result, a majority of the scholarships that are available on the culinary rituals of the South African Indians have primarily emerged from the Hindu kitchen spaces and then, with time, have intertwined with the culinary spaces of the Muslims, Christians, Colored, Cape Malays, Zulus, Bantus, and other communities in South Africa.

However, at present, South African Indian culinary practices cannot be restricted within specific social, cultural, religious, and geographical enclaves. It is true that many high-caste Hindu passenger Indians, in order to preserve their religious puritanism, try to continue with their traditional Indian vegetarian culinary practices because the "practice of vegetarianism is often intimately connected with a striving for respectability" (Diesel 2007, p. 71). But, on many occasions, the high-caste Indians are compelled to adopt creolized culinary cultures due to the lack of availability of local Indian groceries. For instance, Anita, a high-caste Indian woman, who traces her ancestry from the city of Mathura in North India and works as a caretaker in the Luxmi Narayan Temple at Chatsworth, Durban shared that she often serves vegetable *Breyani* (Figure 12) and hot chocolate to the devotees, which is unusual in any Hindu temple in India (2022). On the one side, she did not forget to boast the spiritual superiority of the Brahman-centric Hindu temples over other Hindu temples in Durban; on the other side, she also admitted that it is not always possible to adhere to the Hindu puritan practices due to the "unavailability of local Indian spiritual and culinary ingredients" (Anita 2022). As discussed in Chapter 3, Ravi Govender from the Sithambar Alayam Temple shared an identical story of how the local culinary ingredients of South Africa blended with traditional Indian culinary ingredients to give birth to creole temple foods.

Historically, the adaptation of local Bantu and Zulu culinary practices by the Indian indentured laborers in the sugarcane plantations was also motivated by the crises of a majority of traditional Indian spices and other culinary ingredients. The food items that were supplied as rations in the plantations were deficient in proteins, and as a result, the Indian laborers banked on gizzards, livers, feet, tails, heart, brain, and other animal body parts, that were discarded by the colonial plantation owners, to avoid malnourishment and meet their dietary requirements (Hansen 2013, p. 95). As Maureen Swan in her article "The 1913 Natal Indian Strike" observes that the plantation workers were overworked (as much as seventeen or eighteen hours a day during overlapping, crushing, and planting seasons), subjected to "malnourishment," and poorly housed (1984, p. 243).

The consumption of these animal body parts has been a traditional aspect of Bantu and Zulu culinary cultures in South Africa, and as a result, many South African Indian dishes like Spicy Tripe Curry, *Chettinad* Trotter Curry, Sheep Head Curry, and many others are rooted in Zulu and Bantu dishes like boiled tripe, trotter soup, and saucy tripe curry. The Indians learned to prepare these dishes from their Zulu and Bantu counterparts in the plantations, and to preserve the traditional Indian flavors, they mixed local Indian spices that they managed to bring from India and grow around their living areas in Durban (Marie 2022).

**Figure 12:** Indian-veg biryani with traditional southern African beetroot salad.

Besides dietary crises, linguistic crises were another prominent reason that facilitated the culinary exchanges between the Indians, Zulus, and Bantus in the plantations. For these communities, food served as a language and enabled them to converse with each other in "a dialogue both fundamental and profound" (Accone 2004, p. 1). Prior to learning each other's languages, it was through food that these communities interacted and dreamt together of resistance and freedom from the oppressive working conditions. On the one side, these culinary practices functioned as "vehicles for telling personal or communal experience and for the imagination of senses of selfhood" (Ojwang 2013, p. 73) and on the other side, the practices established physical and emotional "connectedness with one another" (Govinden 2017, p. 46). This simultaneous performance of selfhood and connectedness by the South African Indians through food during the era of slavery and apartheid has continued into postapartheid South Africa by acknowledging the multiracial and multicultural dimensions of a diasporic Indianness in the forms of writing cookbooks, opening restaurants, and selling homemade snacks.

### Creolization as a Multiracial and Multicultural Acknowledgment

The public practice of culinary creolization by the South African Indians began mostly during the early 90s, when the country was chaotically steering toward the end of apartheid. The official end of apartheid in 1994 did not ensure the official end of racial and cultural discrimination in South Africa, but the South African Indians continue to counter the discriminatory practices, and one of the many ways of countering has been through creolizing culinary cultures and generating archipelagoes of tastes. The archipelagoes of tastes open up the South African Indian cultural history to the "porosity of the coastline and the unpredictability of creolization as a cultural process" (Kabir 2022) by understanding culinary tastes as a simultaneous interplay of various patterns of social, cultural, gendered, religious, political, and other cultures that are underpinned by multiple levels of historical exchanges. Like the coexistence of a group of islands in an archipelago, the creolized coexistence of traditional Indian culinary cultures and the local South African culinary cultures have been "unpredictable, chaotic, but ongoing" (Kabir 2022, p. 210). To further understand the public practice of creolized culinary cultures by the South African Indians in the contemporary era, let us look into a few creolized food items and the various sociohistorical factors that have shaped them.

### Afronad Cuisine

The *Afronad* cuisine, according to Bobby Marie, is a creolization of traditional South African and *Chettinad* (Tamil) cuisines. Bobby, a 49-year-old man and a resident of Johannesburg, traces his ancestry from Tamil Nadu and Andhra Pradesh, and during personal conversations he shared that his grandparents, who arrived in South Africa in 1890, tried hard to maintain their association with traditional culinary practices through local Indian spices and the seeds of fruits and vegetables that they brought from India across the Indian Ocean to South Africa. But, due to hostile travel conditions, challenging weather conditions, and fatal living conditions, a lot of the spices and the seeds got rotten (Marie 2022). So, along with whatever local Indian spices could be brought and grown, Bobby's grandparents and other indentured Indians, were compelled to depend on the monthly ration supplies and adopt traditional South African culinary customs from their Bantu and Zulu coworkers. In due course, the simultaneous association of indentured Indians with local Indian spices and South African culinary customs generated a "collective geographical imaginary" (Boatca and Parvulescu 2020, pp. 15–16) in the forms of food items like "Spicy Mango Achar and Pap, Mealie Rice and Dhal, Achaar Chutney, *Kalli*, Sour Porridge, *Kanji Keerai Dhal*, and others" (Marie 2022).

In order to further understand the creolization of local South African and traditional Indian culinary cultures in the abovementioned dishes, let us look at the ways in which the dishes are prepared. Spicy Mango Achaar is a traditional Indian preparation of mango pickles, and Pap is a traditional southern African maize meal; Mealie Rice is an alternative version of Pap, and Dhal is traditionally Indian; Achar Chutney is a mild and condensed preparation of spicy Indian pickles and is made with tomato, raw mango, and local South African herbs; *Kalli* is a southern Indian version of Pap and is made with powdered maize, fried mustard, and curry leaves; sour porridge is a southern Indian version of the traditional fermented maize drink of the Zulus and is made with fermented maize, chopped onion, ginger, tamarind, and curry leaves; and *Kanji Keerai Dhal* is prepared with black lentils, spinach, chopped onion, garlic, and local southern African sour herbs (*Kanji Keerai*).

The creolized character of the *Afronad* cuisine is further understood through the observations of Devarakshanam Govinden (popularly known as Aunt Betty), who is an 80-year-old woman from Durban. During our conversations, she shared that Afro-Indian creole food is not only about "fusion tastes" (Govinden 2022), but also about "social networks, and most meaningful, about interaction" (Pahl and Rowsell 2010, p. 25). Some of the creolized food items that she grew up with are Egg Curry with Tripe, *Madumbi Curry* and *Samp Curry*. The culture of consuming tripe (stomach of the cow) is traditional to the Zulus and Bantus. This culture has been historically adopted by the Indian indentured workers from their African co-workers on the plantation farms and has been interwoven with local Indian culinary preparations like Egg Curry and others. *Madumbi* is a type

**Figure 13:** Indian-styled spicy lamb curry with traditional southern African-styled madumbi (yam).

of Yam that locally grows in South Africa and other parts of southern Africa, and *Madumbi* Curry is prepared with chopped onions, tomatoes, garlic, ginger, curry leaves, five-spice powder, and other Indian spices (Figure 13). *Samp* is a traditional southern African food that consists of pounded and chopped dried corn kernels. Usually, the southern Africans consume *Samp* by soaking it in water. The South African Indians prepare *Samp* Curry by mixing water-soaked *Samp* with traditional Indian spices (Figure 14).

### Durban-Indian Cuisine

Besides the *Afronad* cuisine, the creolization of South African and Indian food habits can also be located within a wider culinary framework of Durban-Indian cuisines, which resulted from the interaction of the southern Indians, Zulus, and Bantus with the Indian community from other parts of India who came to South Africa not only as indentured laborers but also as passenger Indians. As Ishay Govender notes, "The Indian cuisines in South Africa are mostly an outcome of crises and adaptations" (2022). Ishay also shares how dishes like Live Chicken Curry, *Puri Pata*, and Herbs Curry are an outcome of multiple levels of interactions between Indians from different religious and communal groups, the Zulus and the Bantus. Usually, in the Zulu and Bantu culinary traditions, a matured chicken with eggs inside is skinned, roasted, and consumed. The Live Chicken Curry is an Indian adaptation of

**Figure 14:** Indian-styled beans curry prepared with local South African sauces.

this culinary practice, where after roasting a full chicken with eggs, a spicy curry with traditional Indian spices is prepared.

*Puri Pata* evolved in South Africa centrally with the arrival of passenger Indians from Gujarat (Govender 2022). This dish is a creole of Gujarati and Zulu culinary elements. The dish is prepared with chickpea flour and *Madumbi* leaves. The chickpea flour is spiced with five spice powder, cumin powder, and coriander powder and mixed with the *Madumbi* leaves. The thick mixture of flour and *Madumbi* leaves are spiraled and then placed between two flattened deep-fried breads known as *Puri*. The spiraled *Pata* is similar to the traditional Gujarati spiral-shaped snacks known as Patras, which are prepared with *Colcocasia* leaves, chickpea flour, spices, and sweet and sour flavors.

Besides Live Chicken Curry and *Puri Pata*, the creolized culinary cultures of the South African Indians can also be located within food items like Corn Samosa [a samosa made with minced corn, which is predominantly a southern African culinary practice (Naidoo 2022)], *Amasi* Raita [*Amasi* is a sour milk (traditionally consumed by the Zulus and Bantus) and is mixed with chopped onions, cucumbers, tomatoes and fried spices (Naidoo 2022)], Chakalaka [chopped carrots and beans cooked in Indian spices, tomato puree, and green chilies (Naidoo 2022)] (Figure 15), *Madumbi* Kabab Pilau [minced *Madumbi* Kebabs are mixed with traditional Indian spices (Mayat 1998, p. 35)], *Afriki Yakhni* Pilau [made with local southern African herbs, minced chicken, and Indian spices (Mayat, p. 38)], *Dajela* Achar [powdered maize mixed with traditional Indian pickles (Mayat, p. 261)], and others.

## Culinary Creolization as Racial and Cultural Emancipation

These creolized culinary practices of the African diaspora in India and the Indian diaspora in South Africa have been functioning as "a symbol of defiance" (Chetty 2022, p. 1) against the various racial, social, and cultural hierarchies and acknowledging the "fluid boundaries between past and present, scared and secular, 'nature' and culture, and particularly life and death" (Rich 2021, p. 14). The Apartheid era in South Africa and the European colonial era in India have dehumanized, stigmatized, and marginalized these diaspora communities as much as possible. Along with the creolized spiritual and musical cultures, the creolized culinary cultures have enabled these diaspora communities to "intersect and intermingle" (Govinden 2017, p. 132) and develop an "inter-diaspora approach" (Govinden, p. 132) to reread the existing social, cultural, and historical narratives across the world.

The diverse creole foods and the transoceanic, multi-rooted, and transcultural culinary ingredients and sociocultural perspectives that are used to prepare those foods allow us to understand "creolization as balancing act—between oceans, between empires, between metropole and colony, and between different groups of divergently—(dis)empowered people" (Kabir 2020, p. 140). Similar to the creolized spiritual and musical practices, the creolized culinary habits of the Siddis and the South African Indians function as a tool

**Figure 15:** Atchalaka (a mixture of Indian mango pickle and the traditional chakalaka sauce of South Africa).

of racial and cultural emancipation by inviting diverse communities across India, South Africa, and other parts of the world to taste and adopt their cross-cultural cuisines. When different individuals are introduced to the culinary rituals of these communities, the processes of racial and cultural emancipation can be located through the ways in which predetermined cultural imageries get erased, cultural stereotypes get demolished, sociohistorical relationships in connection with "ecological spaces like the ocean" (Mohulatsi 2023, p. 128) get reshaped, and the "aquatic environment" (Mohulatsi, p. 128) gets reimagined as a borderless, permeable, fluid, and porous space of polyvalent knowledge movements.

In order to publicize the creolized culinary practices, the Siddis and South African Indians have been undertaking multiple initiatives, like during *Urs*, when the Siddis invite other communities to attend the festivals and dine with them, and the South African Indians promote their foods through weekend food markets, home restaurants, and cookbooks. The food markets, restaurants, and cookbooks are habitually accessed by communities across diverse races and classes in South Africa, which allows the South African Indians to preserve their Indian ancestral culinary values on the one side, and interact with various traditional southern African culinary patterns on the other. These initiatives may not be the ultimate solutions to the racial and cultural discriminations that these communities have been historically experiencing, but the collective resistance needs to start somewhere, and what better can be done than performing resistance in invitational, respectful, and palatable ways?

## Endnote

1   The phrase can be roughly translated into English as "What is happening? / This is happening." It is sung to acknowledge the spiritual contributions of Mai Misra, for whose blessings the Siddis are able to prepare khichdi and offer it to her.

## References

Accone, D. 2004. *All Under Heaven: The Story of a Chinese Family in South Africa*. Cape Town: David Philip Publishers.

Al-Mubrik, F. and Siddi, H. 2022. 'About Mai Misra's Khichdi and Bava Gor's *Ghava*'. Personal Communication. Bhavnagar.

Anita. 2022. 'About Hindu Temple Food in South Africa'. Personal Conversation. Durban.

Baderoon, G. 2014. *Regarding Muslims: From Slavery to Post-apartheid*. Johannesburg: Wits University Press.

Boatca, M. and Parvulescu, A. 2020. 'Creolizing Transylvania: Notes on Coloniality and Inter-imperiality'. *History of the Present* 10, no. 1: 9–27.

Breteque, P.A. de la. 2021. 'Creolization as Cultural and Poetic Rebirth in "Arrival of the Snake Woman" by Olive Senior'. *Commonwealth Essays and Studies* 44, no. 1: 1–17.

Chetty, R. 2022. *Fatima Meer: Choosing to be Defiant*. Pietermaritzburg: Otterley Press.

Diesel, A. 2007. *Shakti: Stories of Indian Women in South Africa*. Johannesburg: Wits University Press.

dos Anjos, M. 2008. 'Where All Places Are'. In *Cildo Meireles*, edited by Guy Brett, 170–173. London: Tate Modern.

Ghosh, R. 2021. 'The Plastic Turn'. *Diacritics* 49, no. 1: 64–85.

Govender, I. 2022. 'About Afro-Indian Creole Foods in South Africa'. Personal Conversation. Cape Town.

Govinden, B. 2022. 'About Afro-Indian Creole Foods in South Africa'. Personal Conversation. Durban.

Govinden, D. 2017. 'Not Just an Object: Exploring Epistemological Vantages in Postcolonial Thinking'. In *Object Medleys: Interpretive Possibilities for Educational Research*, edited by Daisy Pillay, 45–60. Leiden: Brill.

Graves, J. 2008. 'Mai Misra's *Khicari*: Remembrance and Ritual Re-presentation in the Sidi (African-Indian) Sufi Tradition of Western India'. *Symposia* 9, Special Issue: 1–13.

Hansen, T.B. 2013. *Melancholia of Freedom: Social Life in an Indian Township in South Africa*. Johannesburg: Wits University Press.

Kabir, A.J. 2020. 'Creolization as Balancing Act in the Transoceanic Quadrille: Choreogenesis, Incorporation, Memory, Market'. *Atlantic Studies* 17, no. 1: 135–157.

Kabir, A.J. 2022. 'Creole Indias, Creolizing Pondicherry: Ari Gautier's Le thinnai as the Archipelago of Fragments'. *Comparative Literature* 74, no. 2: 202–218.

Kabir, A.J. 2023. 'The Creolizing Turn and Its Archipelagic Directions'. *The Cambridge Journal of Postcolonial Literary Enquiry*, 1–14, doi:10.1017/pli.2022.31.

Marie, B. 2022. 'About Afro-Indian Creole Foods in South Africa'. Personal Conversation. Johannesburg.

Mayat, Z. 1998. *Indian Delights*. Wandsbeck: Women's Cultural Group.

Mohulatsi, M. 2023. 'Black Aesthetics and Deep Water: Fish-People, Mermaid Art and Slave Memory in South Africa'. *Journal of African Cultural Studies* 35, no. 1: 121–133.

Naidoo, P. 2022. 'About Afro-Indian Creole Foods in South Africa'. Personal Conversation. Durban.

Ojwang, D. 2013. *Reading Migration and Culture: The World of East African Indian Literature*. London & New York: Palgrave Macmillan.

Pahl, K. and Rowsell, J. 2010. *Artifactual Literacies: Every Object Tells a Story*. New York: Teachers College Press.

Rich, S.A. 2021. *Shipwreck Hauntography: Underwater Ruins & the Uncanny*. Amsterdam: Amsterdam University Press.

Swan, M. 1984. 'The 1913 Natal Indian Strike'. *Journal of Southern African Studies* 10, no. 2: 239–258.

Whitehorsepress. 2018. 'Elusive Traces: African Baobabs in India'. *Whitehorsepress*. 2 May. https://whitehorsepress.blog/2018/05/02/elusive-traces-african-baobabs-in-india/.

# Chapter 6

# CONTINUITY: WEAVING ARCHIPELAGOES OF RESISTANCE

The Indian Ocean, like the winds and the storms, cannot be restricted within frontiers. From 1500 to 1800, the Indian Ocean rim included all areas between the Red Sea and the Straits of Malacca. In the 20th century, "Australia and Southern Africa were added" to the Indian Ocean space (Khader 2017, p. 85). Gabeba Baderoon in her book *Regarding Muslims* (2014), argues that "the sea is a metaphor for experiences that transcend conventional categories, the juxtaposition of multiple histories, the transformation of the self, and memories of slavery" (p. 67). On a similar note, this book has reinterpreted the Indian Ocean space through the creolized culinary, spiritual, and musical memories and rituals of the African Indians in Gujarat and the South African Indians in South Africa. The fluidity of the Indian Ocean has generated fluid sociocultural practices amongst the communities residing in and around that space, as can be seen in the cases of the African Indians and the South African Indians. The various sociocultural creolized practices of the African Indians and the South African Indians, as discussed in this book, have pushed these communities into a state of "informed accommodation," which Khatija Khader defines as a practice by communities to mark a distinct identity "by claiming membership into other larger regional or global groups— to mark similarity" (2020, p. 438). During personal conversations, the African Indians and the South African Indians shared their habitual culinary and spiritual and the musical practices that enable them to remember their "distinctive" ancestral practices, on the one side, and identify "similarities" between the sociocultural practices of the local Indian and African communities, respectively, on the other. The African Indians in Gujarat, while respecting their relationship to the local Indian cultures and traditions, never fail to acknowledge their connections to African ancestry. On a similar note, a lot of South African Indians identify their distinctiveness from the rest of the South Africans by simultaneously acknowledging their Indian and South African roots. These dynamics of informed accommodation can be thoroughly understood through the theoretical and ethnographic narratives of the struggles and resistances of the African Indians and the South African Indians. The multi-rooted sociocultural practices of these communities have led to the formation of several diaspora spaces across the Indian Ocean (Baron and Cara 2011). With respect to the phenomenon of diaspora space, Avtar Brah, in his book *Cartographies of Diaspora* (1996), emphasizes that the concept of diaspora is not limited to singular historical experience (p. 18). Rather, the phenomenon of diaspora expands across diverse "maps and histories" in a complex and interwoven manner (Brah 1996, p. 25). The narratives in this book also unpack the ways in which these diasporic communities, through informed accommodation in their respective diaspora spaces, are making consistent efforts to shift their existential positionalities and experiences from "liminal diaspora" toward "flexible diaspora" by constructing senses of "affiliation across borders" (Govinden 2008, p. 182). The creolized sociocultural practices allow the African Indians and the South African Indians to gain "freedom from spatial constraints," to generate possibilities of "archipelagic belonging and transoceanic worlding" (Wilson 2022, p. 5) and to build archives of "deterritorialized resources" (Ong 1999, p. 16). The archives of deterritorialized resources make a consistent effort to challenge the spatial, temporal, and geographical enclaves of the mainstream sociocultural practices of India and South Africa.

In addition to the discussions in Chapter 2 about the liminal diasporic experiences of the African Indian community in Gujarat and the South African Indian community in South Africa, it is important to note that the experiences of otherness, difference, precarity, and alterity are systematically preserved and acknowledged through distorting histories, spreading sociopolitical rumors, inventing racialized narratives, and erasing archives. During my field research in South Africa, I visited the Workers Museum in Johannesburg, which has archived the torturous experiences of the black miners in South Africa during the European colonial era through photographs, letters, and objects. I was astonished to see that despite the massive contribution of the Indian indentured laborers toward the development of the mining industry in South Africa, nothing has been mentioned about them. Museum Africa in Johannesburg also portrays an identical picture. The section in which the museum displays stories about Indian contributions in the anti-apartheid movement is underlined with cultural, racial, caste, and political hierarchies. The section mostly centers on Gandhi and his close associate of passenger Indians, with a little recognition of the resistance movements and the mass mobilization activities of the indentured Indian community. Kwa Muhle Museum and Local History Museum in Durban are no different. In these museums, the histories of Indians are underrepresented and are exclusively woven around Gandhi and Gandhi-centric activities in South

Africa. These museums claim to represent the history of the lives and works of the local natives of Durban, but except for a photograph of a burnt Indian shop during the Cato Manor riots in 1959 (in the Kwa Buhle Museum) and idols of Hajee Malukmahomed Lappa Sultan[1] and Mahatma Gandhi (in Local History Museum), no information about the Indian community in South Africa can be found.

However, a detailed public archive of the social, cultural, and historical contributions of the Indian indentured community exists in South Africa, and it can only be located in the 1860 Heritage Centre in Durban, which consists of their stories, photographs, and objects (musical instruments, garments, utensils, etc.). Besides permanent exhibitions, the heritage center regularly organizes special exhibitions on the cultural contributions of the Indian indentured communities in South Africa. But the existence of this center to archive the histories of the South African Indians is not sufficient because the narratives remain restricted within a particular physical space. Though there is a website that outlines the details about the center, but it is not possible to display every exhibit of the center on the website due to various ethical and copyright issues. Therefore, to access the complete archive, it is necessary to physically visit the center in Durban. Also, the center mostly covers the history of the indentured Indian community in Durban. A majority of the historical narratives about the Indian communities in other parts of South Africa have remained undocumented and ignored. This systemic, epistemic, and ontological ignorance of the sociopolitical contributions of the Indian indentured laborers have permanently marginalized, demonized, and stigmatized the community in the country. This is why Thomas Blom Hansen, in his book *Melancholia of Freedom* (2012), rightly points out that "the perception of Indians [especially the indentured Indians] as a culturally alien, unreliable, and opportunistic minority has a long history among both white and African communities in South Africa" (p. 26).

The liminal diasporic experiences of the African Indians in Gujarat are quite identical to those of the South African Indians. Similar to the Indian community in South Africa, the African Indians in Gujarat and widely in India are subjected to varied forms of social, cultural, racial, communal, religious, economic, and political marginalization. Besides poor access to basic infrastructural facilities like education, health, and jobs, the sociohistorical narratives of the African Indians in Gujarat are hardly reflected in the colonial and postcolonial archives of Indian history. A majority of the history books do not talk about the African-Indian community in India. There are a few history books that just mention their presence in India. Over the last couple of decades, though a few history books on the social, cultural, and economic practices of the African Indian community in India have been written, but they are not taught in the school and university syllabuses. Moreover, the history books mostly present the African Indian community in a very stereotypical and romanticized manner by exclusively focusing on their music and dance, without talking about their habitual struggles and existential concerns. It is also important to unpack the internal hierarchies within the African Indian community in India. The African Indians, who trace their origins to the royal African families of Janjira in Maharashtra and Sachin in Gujarat, often look down upon the rest of the African Indians who have originated from the slave community and invalidate their Africanness. This could be thoroughly understood through the socioeconomic disparities between these two groups of African Indians. While the African Indians from the royal lineage have comfortable access to education and jobs, the African Indians from the slave lineage struggle for the same. The museums in India are also ignorant about the sociohistorical contribution of the African Indians, who originated from the slaves.

These systemic ways of ignoring and oppressing the sociohistorical contributions of the South African Indians and the African Indians are being countered by their creolized sociohistorical practices. The creolized sociocultural practices are gradually transforming the liminal diasporic experiences of these communities toward flexible diasporic experiences, which acknowledge and appreciate their multi-rootedness, although they are geographically located in a particular physical location. The flexible diasporic experiences are nurturing these communities as what Engseng Ho identifies as "mobile cosmopolitans" (2002, p. 218). The term refers to the trading communities, indentured laborers, and minorities who have traveled with the European colonial empires across the globe. The aspect of mobile cosmopolitanism gets reflected in the transoceanic, racially interwoven, and socioculturally creolized practices of African Indian and the South African Indian communities. Historically, along with and beyond the European colonial empires, these communities have "moved within a conception of space that [is] not unitary and a representation of identity that [is] not localized even if territorially rooted" (Khader 2017, p. 85). The nonlinear, porous, and mobile existence of these communities has forged their creolized spiritual, culinary, and musical practices that we find today.

It is necessary to document and archive the creolized sociocultural practices, not only to interrogate the misrepresentations of the Siddis and the South African Indians in particular, but also to interrogate the misrepresentation, misinterpretation, and demonization of the Indian Ocean World by the navigators, scientists, geographers, theorists, and philosophers in general. Pliny, Strabo, Christopher Columbus, Vasco da Gama, and many others have distorted the Indian Ocean spaces by identifying wrong directions, identifying wrong geographical locations, naming communities in an assimilative manner, and in various other ways. This short book is "an"-other effort to interrogate these distortions and unpack diverse creolized sociocultural performances as a possibility of resisting such problematic narratives and building transoceanic archives across the Indian Ocean World. Through discussing the creolized spiritual, culinary, and the musical practices of the Siddis and the South African Indians, this book documents how these communities are making a shift from experiences of "painful remembering" toward a collaborative remembering (Bhabha 1994, p. 63). The habitual performances of the diaspora communities reflect how their bodies are simultaneously intersected with "location and dislocation—of an uprooting and a transplanting in distant and strange soils" (Ratnam 2019). The book also analyzes how experiences of "alienated reconciliation" of the African Indians and South African Indians, which is about trying to geopolitically and socioculturally locate the roots; failing to locate the roots or feeling alienated from the so-called geopolitical and sociocultural roots, and then shifting closer to the diaspora spaces, have given birth to their creolized sociocultural practices.

The liminal sociohistorical experiences across the Indian Ocean present the Indian Ocean as an "archipelago of fragments" (Kabir and Gautier 2022a). The Indian Ocean as an archipelago of fragments challenges the linear process of knowledge production across the globe by putting together the creolized bits and pieces of the cultural practices of different diaspora communities across the world, as can be seen in the cases of Siddis and South African Indians. The creolized sociocultural practices of the African Indians and the South African Indians (especially the indentured laborers) have generated "in-between spaces of resistance through collaboration" (Kabir and Gautier 2022b, p. 55) and powerful archives of peacebuilding and decolonial healing. The discussions about their sociocultural performances in this book "urge towards cross-cultural dialogue without the baggage of imperialism" (Chakrabarty 2005, p. 4812). The book also makes efforts to establish "new interdisciplinary, transregional, and transoceanic conversations" (Kabir 2023, p. 14) on the phenomenon of creolization.

For a further understanding of the sociocultural practices of these communities, besides making documentaries, writing research articles, and books, it is crucial to introduce the histories of these communities in the school and university curriculums in India, South Africa, and other countries. The introduction of their histories in the schools and universities would enable the people to get acquainted with their creolized diversities on the one side, and to bulldoze the mainstream, compartmentalized, hierarchical, dominant, and elitist Eurocentric historical narratives on the other. The act of bulldozing the dominant and compartmentalized Eurocentric narratives will also entitle the communities in and around the Indian Ocean to socially, culturally, politically, geographically, and cartographically weave depolarized, plural, and creolized spaces of deeply entangled knowledge systems.

The conversations do not conclude here. As the book needs to stop somewhere, so, the discussions briefly pause for the readers to contemplate, analyze, and "reopen the past for reflection in order to make moments of liberation possible in the future" (Chen 2010, p. 10).

## Endnote

1   An educationist and social activist whose parents came to Durban from Gujarat. He was also a close associate of Mahatma Gandhi.

## References

Baderoon, G. 2014. *Regarding Muslims: From Slavery to Post-apartheid*. Johannesburg: Wits University Press.

Baron, R. and Cara, A.C. 2011. 'Introduction: Creolization as Cultural Creativity'. In *Creolization as Cultural Creativity*, edited by R. Baron and A.C. Cara, 3–19. Mississippi: University Press of Mississippi.

Bhabha, H.K. 1994. *The Location of Culture*. London and New York: Routledge.

Brah, A. 1996. *Cartographies of Diaspora: Contesting Identities*. London and New York: Routledge.

Chakrabarty, D. 2005. 'Legacies of Bandung'. *Economic and Political Weekly* 40, no. 46: 4812–4818.

Chen, K-H. 2010. *Asia as Method: Toward Deimperialization*. Durham and London: Duke University Press.

Govinden, D.B. 2008. *A Time of Memory: Reflections on Recent South African Writings*. Durban: Solo Collective.

Hansen, T.B. 2012. *Melancholia of Freedom: Social Life in an Indian Township in South Africa*. Johannesburg: Wits University Press.

Ho, E. 2002. 'Names Beyond Nations: The Making Cosmopolitans'. *Etudesrurales* 163/164: 215–231.

Kabir, A.J. and Gautier, A. 2022a. *Le Thinnai Creole* [Facebook]. 29 April. Available at: https://www.facebook.com/watch/live/?ref=watch_permalink&v=675487460412399 (Accessed 20 May 2022).

Kabir, A.J. and Gautier, A. 2022b. 'Creolisation in Pondicherry: The Superfluous Necessity'. *Zist* 23: 54–62.

Kabir, A.J. 2023. 'The Creolizing Turn and Its Archipelagic Directions'. *The Cambridge Journal of Postcolonial Literary Enquiry* 10, no. 1: 1–14.

Khader, K. 2017. 'Mobile Communities of the Indian Ocean: A Brief Study of Siddi and Hadrami Diaspora in Hyderabad City, India'. In *Global Africans: Race, Ethnicity and Shifting Identities*, edited by T. Falola and C. Hoyer, 76–93. New York: Routledge.

Khader, K.S. 2020. 'Translocal Notions of Belonging and Authenticity: Understanding Race amongst the Siddis of Gujarat and Hyderabad'. *South Asian History and Culture* 11, no. 4: 433–448.

Ong, A. 1999. *Flexible Citizenship: The Cultural Logics of Transnationality*. Durham: Duke University Press.

Ratnam, A.R. 2019. Foreword to *Bharathanatyam: An Ancient Indian Classical Dance: A Journey from India to South Africa*, by Vasugi Dewar Singh, i–iii. Durban: Atlas Printers.

Wilson, R.S. 2022. 'Introduction: Worlding Asia Pacific into Oceania – Worlding Concepts, Tactics, and Transfigurations against the Anthropocene'. In *Geo-Spatiality in Asian and Oceanic Literature and Culture: Worlding Asia in the Anthropocene*, edited by S.S. Chou et al., 1–31. Ithaca: Cornell University Press.

# AFTERWORD

The primary question dealt with in this book—whether identities are fixed or do they travel across economies, geographies, epistemologies, and ontologies?—reminds me of Sara Shneiderman's (2015) question of "is ethnicity a rock or a river?" (p. 3) While looking at how ethnicity as an identity is understood and practiced among the Thangmi community in Nepal and parts of India, she underlined that while community members, to gain state recognition of their ethnicity, performed ethnicity in a way that led to the framing of their identity as a fixed object, deep down in the community's consciousness, ethnicity was truly processual—never in a state of being but always becoming (Anthias 2006; Bhambra 2006).

Framing identity as a "rock" or as a fixed object leads to the reification of identities, something that Nancy Fraser (2000) warned us against while talking about the "identity model." Consequently, one can experience blockages and disruptions to the flows, of intermingling between identities and cultures, which Dey has touched upon when he writes about the racial discrimination faced by African Indians in Gujarat or when he discusses how caste consciousness among upper-caste Hindus in South Africa leads to their racist behavior toward local black Africans. This book, thus, comes at an important time when identities are increasingly being turned into fixed entities and are politicized—the rise of right-wing fascist regimes all over the world is an indication of that.

In such a world, Dey in turn decides to focus on the "porosity and hybridity," the flows, and "non-purity." This has allowed the work to open up discussions surrounding belongingness, which is in line with scholars such as Deleuze and Guattari (1987) and Yuval-Davis (2011). Deleuze and Guattari (1987) question fixity, linearity, cyclical, and binary thought-processes, including belongingness, by placing the image of the root, which is always "tracing" origins, goes in one linear direction, and works with binary logic, in opposition to the image of the "rhizome." As opposed to the "root," the rhizome is nonlinear, multiplies in any direction, and works with the principles of connection and heterogeneity. The rhizome does not reproduce like tracing in exact ways; it is a map that draws unique connections and is opposed to any fixed structure. A root reterritorializes, but a rhizome deterritorializes, and then it may again reterritorialize and again deterritorialize, and this goes on without any order. Dey reflects this when he evokes the term "multi-rootedness." While talking about the diasporic communities in India and South Africa, he writes, "The creolized socio-cultural practices are gradually transforming the liminal diasporic experiences of these communities toward flexible diasporic experiences, which acknowledge and appreciate their multi-rootedness, although they are geographically located in a particular physical location." This, he exemplifies, through talking about creolized cultures surrounding food, music, and spirituality/religion amongst the diasporic communities of African Indians and Indian South Africans.

Dey's appreciation and fascination with flows, transcultural and transoceanic processes can be traced to his own migratory history. The work being truly reflexive, Dey clarifies his positionality by talking about his family and lineage. His grandparents' migrating from present-day Bangladesh during the 1971 Bangladesh Liberation War to India's West Bengal region and the passing down of little-known historical knowledge surrounding the migratory history of other communities within the family (African kingdom in Bengal in 15th century) have contributed in their own way to Dey's interest toward intermingling and heterogeneity.

The fact that his own "roots" are sprinkled across many "origin points" surpassing national borders (besides spending his childhood in Kolkata, Maldah, Raiganj, his familial roots also exist in Faridpur, Dhaka, Mymensingh, and Chittagong in Bangladesh) has allowed him to not be obsessed with "tracing" identities to one fixed origin point. This has also allowed him to appreciate how the identities of people and communities can expand in any direction, absorbing the local cultures, histories, and sentiments while retaining some of their own. His own history, thus, has allowed him to embody rhizomatic sentimentality.

Thus, one should not be surprised when one finds that Dey's interests and work forward narratives celebrating decoloniality, intersectional ways of preserving life, interracial studies, and in-betweenness. In fact, in the days to come, we will see Dey contributing significantly toward expanding studies on intersectionality and decoloniality, wherein one can experience decolonial writing not simply in its content but also in the entire process of epistemic constructions—from data sources to methodologies and more. This book, alongside Dey's many other works, is simply the beginning of those that embody such sentiments in their truest sense.

**Bhargabi Das**
Assistant Professor, Shiv Nadar University

# References

Anthias, F. 2006. 'Belongings in a Globalising and Unequal World: Rethinking Translocations'. In *The Situated Politics of Belonging*, edited by Nira Yuval-Davis, Kalpana Kannabiran and Ulrike Vieten, 17–31. London: SAGE Publications Ltd.

Bhambra, G.K. 2006. 'Culture, Identity and Rights: Challenging Contemporary Discourses of Belonging'. In *The Situated Politics of Belonging*, edited by Nira Yuval-Davis, Kalpana Kannabiran and Ulrike Vieten, 32–41. London: SAGE Publications Ltd.

Deleuze, G. and Guattari, F. 1987. *A Thousand Plateaus: Capitalism and Schizophrenia*. Minneapolis: University of Minnesota Press.

Fraser, N. (2000). Rethinking Recognition. *New Left Review* 3: 107–120.

Shneiderman, S. 2015. *Rituals of Ethnicity: Thangmi Identities Between Nepal and India*. Philadelphia: University of Pennsylvania Press.

Yuval-Davis, N. 2011. *The Politics of Belonging: Intersectional Contestations*. London: SAGE Publications Ltd.

# INDEX

Milton Keynes UK
Ingram Content Group UK Ltd.
UKHW041808180224
438062UK00001B/4